The MOST INSPIRING RUGBY STORIES OF ALL TIME

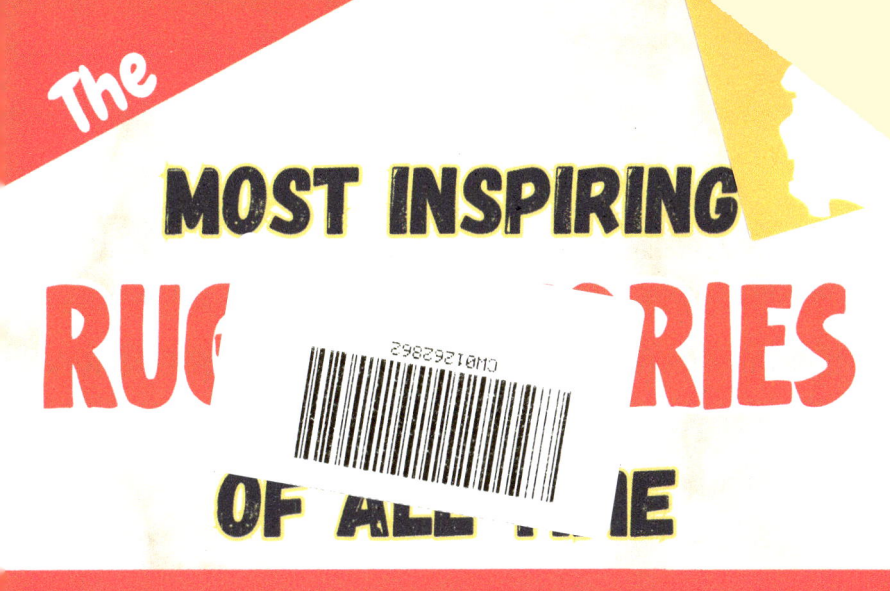

FOR YOUNG READERS

Dr. Fanatomy

© Copyright 2023-24 - All rights reserved.

The content contained within this book may not be reproduced, duplicated or transmitted without direct written permission from the author or the publisher.

Under no circumstances will any blame or legal responsibility be held against the publisher, or author, for any damages, reparation, or monetary loss due to the information contained within this book, either directly or indirectly.

Legal Notice:
This book is copyright protected. It is only for personal use. You cannot amend, distribute, sell, use, quote, or paraphrase any part, or the content within this book, without the author or publisher's consent.

Disclaimer Notice:
Please note the information contained within this document is for educational and entertainment purposes only. All effort has been executed to present accurate, up-to-date, reliable, complete information. No warranties of any kind are declared or implied. Readers acknowledge that the author is not engaged in the rendering of legal, financial, medical or professional advice. The content within this book has been derived from various sources. Please consult a licensed professional before attempting any techniques outlined in this book.

By reading this document, the reader agrees that under no circumstances is the author responsible for any losses, direct or indirect, that are incurred as a result of the use of the information contained within this document, including, but not limited to, errors, omissions, or inaccuracies.

Bonus Booklet For You!

With great pleasure, I warmly welcome you to purchase the book. Congratulations on stepping towards improving yourself and developing the skills necessary to thrive as a teenager and beyond.

Below is a surprise gift for you!

Download it from the link (or scan the QR code below) -
https://bit.ly/TeeNavigationBonus

Table of Contents

Introduction: The World of Rugby (pg 1-5)

- Unearthing the Origins of Rugby
- A Personal Anecdote
- The Passion that Ignites Rugby's Soul
- A Poll for Young Rugby Fans
- Fun Corner 1
- Did You Know

Chapter 1: Legendary Players (pg 6-15)

- Jonny Wilkinson: The Drop Goal that Defined a Generation
- Jonah Lomu: The Unstoppable Force from New Zealand
- Gareth Edwards: The Maestro of Welsh Rugby
- Fun Corner 2
- Did You Know

Chapter 2: Memorable Matches (pg 16-24)

- The 2003 Rugby World Cup Final: England vs. Australia
- The 'Invincible' Tour of the British and Irish Lions
- The 1973 Barbarians vs. All Blacks Match: A Try for the Ages
- Did You Know

Chapter 3: Triumph and Adversity (pg 25-33)

- Martin Johnson: From Captaining England to World Cup Glory
- The Calcutta Cup: England vs. Scotland Rivalry
- David Pocock: Rugby's Advocate for Social Change
- Did You Know

Table of Contents

Chapter 4: Women in Rugby (pg 34-44)

- Emily Scarratt: England's Star on the Rise
- Black Ferns: Dominance in Women's Rugby
- Respect and Equality: The Progress of Women's Rugby
- Did You Know

Chapter 5: Underdog Stories (pg 45-54)

- Japan's Historic Upset: Rugby World Cup 2015
- The 'Swing Low, Sweet Chariot' England Anthem
- The Legacy of Richie McCaw: A Rugby Hero
- Did You Know

Chapter 6: Young Rugby Heroes (pg 55-67)

- Billy Vunipola: A Rising Star in English Rugby
- James O'Connor: From Young Sensation to Redemption
- The Future Stars: Aspiring Young Rugby Talents
- Did You Know

Table of Contents

Chapter 7: Inspiring Coaches and Mentors (pg 68-78)

- Sir Clive Woodward: Shaping England's Success
- Sir Graham Henry: The All Blacks' Mastermind
- Eddie Jones: England's Strategic Leader
- Did You Know

Chapter 8: The Global Rugby Family (pg 79-91)

- The Spirit of Rugby World Cups
- The Passion of the Six Nations
- The Thrill of the Rugby Championship
- Did You Know

Chapter 9: Fun Corner: Quiz (pg 92-100)

Conclusion (pg 101)

INTRODUCTION

Welcome to a thrilling adventure into the world of Rugby, where history, passion, and camaraderie come together to create a unique sport that has captured the hearts of millions across the globe.

Unearthing the Origins of Rugby

Our journey begins with a glimpse into the past, revealing that Rugby's origins are far more intriguing than the average sports fan might imagine. The story commences in the early 19th century in a charming English town named Rugby. During a conventional soccer match at Rugby School, a student, <u>William Webb Ellis</u>, had a moment of inspiration. Instead of merely kicking the ball as tradition dictated, he daringly picked it up and ran with it, thus giving birth to an entirely new game – rugby football.

From its humble inception, Rugby branched into two distinct forms: rugby union and rugby league. The former, characterized by scrums, lineouts, and an emphasis on kicking, is the more traditional version. Conversely, rugby league is a faster-paced, simpler variant. Both, however, have captured the hearts of millions across the globe.

A Personal Anecdote

Growing up in a small town, I was captivated by the sight of my older brother engaged in a thrilling game of Rugby.

The passion, the energy, and the camaraderie in that field were infectious. I couldn't wait to join in the excitement myself.

Webb Ellis, running with the ball in his hand, in front of the Rugby School.
By G-13114 - Own work, CC BY-SA 4.0, https://commons.wikimedia.org/w/index.php?curid=129185384

Once I got my chance, I was hooked. I fell in love with the physicality of the sport, the thrill of sprinting down the field with the ball in hand, and the unparalleled sense of teamwork with my fellow players. Rugby became more than just a sport to me; it became a way of life.

The Passion that Ignites Rugby's Soul

What truly sets Rugby apart is the extraordinary passion it ignites in players and fans alike. It's not merely a game; it's a lifestyle. The sense of camaraderie, the cherished traditions, and the unwavering love for the sport are shared by every rugby devotee. Stepping onto a rugby field isn't just about playing a game; it's about becoming part of a global brotherhood (and sisterhood).

The thunderous roar of the crowd, the stirring national anthems filling the air, and the sight of players giving their all, even in the face of torrential rain, are all part of the indescribable magic of Rugby. It's about passion, resilience, and an unyielding spirit that unites rugby enthusiasts from all walks of life.

Just imagine the electrifying roar of the crowd as the ball is launched into play, the bone-rattling tackles as players collide, and the triumphant cheers as a team score a try. The energy is palpable, the excitement is electric, and the passion is undeniable. That's the experience of being at a rugby match.

A Poll for Young Rugby Fans

Which rugby team do you think is the best in the world?

- All Blacks
- Springboks
- Wallabies
- England
- Wales

Your Answer : ....

Fun Corner 1

Test your rugby knowledge with this quick quiz!

- Which country has won the most Rugby World Cups?

- What is the name of the trophy awarded to the Six Nations Championship winner?

- Who is the all-time leading try scorer in Rugby World Cup history?

Answers at the end of the book

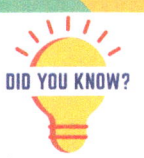

Major Countries and Their Major Cups/Tournaments

major rugby countries and the cups/tournaments they participate in

Country	Major Cups/Tournaments
New Zealand	Rugby World Cup (3 titles), Bledisloe Cup (with Australia), Rugby Championship
Australia	Rugby World Cup (2 titles), Bledisloe Cup (with New Zealand), Rugby Championship
South Africa	Rugby World Cup (3 titles), Mandela Challenge Plate (with Argentina), Rugby Championship
England	Rugby World Cup (1 title), Six Nations Championship, Calcutta Cup (with Scotland)
Ireland	Six Nations Championship, Triple Crown, Centenary Quaich (with Scotland)
Wales	Six Nations Championship, Triple Crown, Centenary Quaich (with Scotland), Calcutta Cup (with England)
France	Six Nations Championship, Giuseppe Garibaldi Trophy (with Italy), Auld Alliance Trophy (with Scotland)
Argentina	Rugby Championship, Puma Trophy (with South Africa)
Scotland	Six Nations Championship, Triple Crown (with England and Ireland), Centenary Quaich (with Ireland), Calcutta Cup (with England), Auld Alliance Trophy (with France)

1. LEGENDARY PLAYERS

- Jonny Wilkinson: The Drop Goal that Defined a Generation
- Jonah Lomu: The Unstoppable Force from New Zealand
- Gareth Edwards: The Maestro of Welsh Rugby

JONNY WILKINSON:
THE DROP GOAL THAT DEFINED A GENERATION

Jonny Wilkinson

Attribution:By David Coldrey from Flickr - originally posted to Flickr as Jonny Wilkinson, CC BY 2.0, https://commons.wikimedia.org/w/index.php?curid=7611095

7

Welcome, young rugby enthusiasts, to the incredible story of Jonny Wilkinson, a name synonymous with passion, precision, and the unforgettable drop goal that shook the rugby world.

Jonny's journey began in Frimley, England, on May 26, 1979. Despite struggling with asthma from a young age, he refused to be held back. He started playing rugby at just six years old, setting the stage for an inspiring tale of perseverance.

What set Jonny apart wasn't just his talent; it was his meticulous approach. He spent countless hours perfecting his kicking technique, earning a reputation for accuracy from any point on the field.

Let's transport ourselves to the historic 2003 Rugby World Cup final. England and Australia were deadlocked at 17-17 in extra time, and the tension was palpable. Then came the moment – a penalty kick awarded to England. Jonny Wilkinson stepped up with nerves of steel. The match's fate rested on his shoulders, but he sent the ball soaring through the uprights with unmatched precision, securing England's first-ever World Cup title.

"It was the most important kick of my life," remarked Jonny Wilkinson. His coach, Clive Woodward, hailed it as "the greatest drop goal ever kicked," while Australia's captain, George Gregan, acknowledged it as "a kick that will be remembered for generations."

But Jonny's story isn't just about that triumphant kick. It's about the early struggles with asthma, the meticulous preparation, and the unwavering mental toughness. His journey inspires young players everywhere to dream big and work hard.

In the echoes of that drop goal, Jonny Wilkinson became not just a rugby player but a symbol of what's possible when passion meets dedication. His story is a testament to the belief that one person can make a difference, and it continues to inspire young rugby players to set their minds on achieving greatness.

So, as you step onto the rugby field, remember Jonny Wilkinson and the drop goal that defined a generation. Let his story be your inspiration, and may it fuel your passion for the game, just as it has for countless others.

JONAH LOMU:
THE UNSTOPPABLE FORCE FROM NEW ZEALAND

Jonah Lomu
By Phil. - bigpip - Jonah Lomu during his short stint at Cardiff Blues, CC BY-SA 2.0.
https://commons.wikimedia.org/w/index.php?curid=7123640

Welcome, future rugby legends! Sit on the grass, grab a snack, and get ready to hear the awe-inspiring tale of one of rugby's all-time greats—Jonah Lomu.

Imagine a young Jonah born in Auckland, New Zealand, on May 12, 1975. From an early age, he showed signs of being destined for greatness in rugby. Despite facing a rare kidney disorder as a child, Jonah overcame his health challenges to become one of the most dominant players in rugby history. At 6'5" and 260 pounds, he was a behemoth on the field, but he was also incredibly fast and agile, able to run like a cheetah and easily tear through defenses.

Jonah's first breakthrough came in 1994 at the Hong Kong Sevens tournament when he was just 19 years old. He burst onto the scene with devastating performances, leaving opponents and fans in disbelief. His unique size, speed, and power made him virtually unstoppable.

Jonah Lomu was special because of his physical prowess, his deep love for the game, and his passion for performing at the highest level. He was a fierce competitor, but he was also a gracious sportsman. On and off the field, Jonah was a role model for young rugby players everywhere.

The 1995 Rugby World Cup was Jonah Lomu's coming-out party. He took the tournament by storm, scoring seven tries in six matches, including four in a single match against England in the semifinals. His performances were so electrifying that he became a global superstar overnight.

Jonah's impact on the game of rugby was immense. He helped to change the way the game was played and inspired a generation of players to follow in his footsteps. He was a true icon of the sport, and his legacy inspires rugby players of all ages today.

In addition to his on-field accomplishments, Jonah Lomu was also a beloved figure off the field. He was known for his humility, kindness, and infectious smile. He was a true ambassador for rugby and a role model for young people everywhere.

Some interesting data points about Jonah Lomu:
- He scored 37 tries in 63 Test matches for New Zealand, the most by any All-Black player.
- He was named IRB World Player of the Year in 1995 and 1997.
- He is the only player to have scored four tries in a single Rugby World Cup match.
- He was inducted into the World Rugby Hall of Fame in 2011.

Jonah Lomu was an exceptional rugby player. He was a physical force, a gifted athlete, and a passionate competitor. But more importantly, he was a role model for young people everywhere. His story is an inspiration to us all.

Waxwork of Lomu in Madame Tussauds London

By https://www.flickr.com/photos/alfahad91/ - https://www.flickr.com/photos/alfahad91/2762164635/, CC BY-SA 2.0, https://commons.wikimedia.org/w/index.php?curid=7107868

GARETH EDWARDS: THE MAESTRO OF WELSH RUGBY

Attention all young rugby enthusiasts! Don your favorite jerseys and bask in the warm glow of the setting sun as we delve into the extraordinary tale of Welsh rugby's maestro, Gareth Edwards. Join us for a captivating story that goes beyond the try line and resonates through the ages.

Gareth Edwards was born in Gwaun-Cae-Gurwen, Wales, on July 12, 1947. He was not just a rugby player but a composer crafting a masterpiece on the field. As a scrum-half, he wielded his skills like a puppeteer, orchestrating moves and dazzling spectators with swift and strategic plays. His passes were the notes in a perfectly tuned melody, seamlessly connecting with his teammates.

In 1971, as part of the British Lions touring New Zealand, Gareth performed a moment of magic. During the second test, he received the ball from JPR Williams, initiating a breathtaking counter-attack. He traversed over 100 meters, weaving through the All Blacks defense before stylishly crossing the try line. This moment in rugby history solidified Gareth's status as a global icon.

Gareth captained Wales to three Grand Slams in the 1970s and earned the title IRB World Player of the Year in 1977. He played 53 Test matches for Wales, scoring 20 tries, and captained Wales 13 times. He was inducted into the World Rugby Hall of Fame. Off the field, Gareth was more than a player; he was a respected and admired figure known for his humility, sportsmanship, and genuine love for the game. His retirement from international rugby in 1978 did not diminish his influence; his legacy lives on, inspiring players and fans alike.

Gareth Edwards remains a true legend, a maestro on the field, and a role model off it. His story is not just about rugby; it inspires us all.

Gareth Edwards:
By Prysiau profile at Flickr website - Flickr original image. CC BY-SA 2.0, https://commons.wikimedia.org/w/index.php?curid=7404419

Sculpture of Gareth Edwards< St. Davids Centre, Cardiff, Wales
By Ruth Sharville, CC BY-SA 2.0, https://commons.wikimedia.org/w/index.php?curid=6007910

Maurice was suspended during a game, which made the fans in Montreal unhappy. However, they remarkably supported him by starting a protest that went down in history as the "Richard Riot." It was a moment when people stood up for their beliefs, significantly impacting the sport and society.

What can we learn from Maurice "The Rocket" Richard? We can learn that no matter how big or small you are and regardless of where you come from, with passion and determination, you can achieve greatness. Maurice's story is a testament to the power of believing in yourself and standing up for what you believe is right.

Furthermore, this is just the beginning of our journey into the world of Canadian hockey legends. We'll uncover more incredible stories of dedication, triumph, and unforgettable moments that continue to inspire the next generation of Canadian hockey players. Are you ready for the next story, my young puck enthusiast?

Fun Corner 2

Test your rugby knowledge with this quick quiz!

- Which Welsh rugby player captained his team to three Grand Slams in the 1970s and is often referred to as "The Maestro of Welsh Rugby"?

- Who is known for his meticulous kicking technique and secured England's victory in the 2003 Rugby World Cup final with a crucial drop goal?

- In 1971, which legendary player scored a breathtaking try during a British Lions tour of New Zealand, covering over 100 meters and weaving through the All Blacks defense?

Answers at the end of the book

DID YOU KNOW?

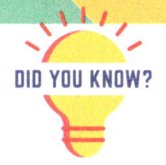

Jonny Wilkinson Trivia:
- Jonny Wilkinson is an English rugby legend and holds the record for being England's all-time leading point-scorer with an impressive 1,246 points.
- At 24, Wilkinson etched his name in rugby history by kicking the winning drop goal in the 2003 Rugby World Cup final against Australia. This iconic moment secured England's first-ever World Cup title.

Jonah Lomu Trivia:
- Hailing from New Zealand, Jonah Lomu became the youngest All-Black at 19 years and 45 days after his debut.
- Lomu's incredible prowess is highlighted by his record-setting 15 tries in Rugby World Cup matches, which still stands as a testament to his dominance on the field.

Gareth Edwards Trivia:
- Gareth Edwards, the Welsh rugby maestro, was celebrated for his extraordinary speed and vision, playing the scrum-half position with unparalleled skill.
- Widely recognized as one of the greatest rugby players ever, Edwards played a pivotal role in the British and Irish Lions' historic series win against New Zealand in 1971—a tour considered among rugby's finest moments.

Rugby World Cup Trivia:
- The inaugural Rugby World Cup took place in 1987 in New Zealand and Australia, with the All Blacks emerging as the first champions in the tournament's history.
- The coveted trophy awarded to the winner of the Rugby World Cup is the Webb Ellis Cup, named in honor of the alleged inventor of rugby.

International Achievements:
- Richie McCaw, former captain of New Zealand, boasts an unparalleled record as the most-capped Test rugby player in history, accumulating an impressive 148 appearances.
- Bryan Habana from South Africa achieved a remarkable feat by securing the record for the most tries in a single Rugby World Cup tournament, scoring eight tries in 2007.

2: MEMORABLE MATCHES

- The 2003 Rugby World Cup Final: England vs. Australia
- The 'Invincible' Tour of the British and Irish Lions
- The 1973 Barbarians vs. All Blacks Match: A Try for the Ages

THE 2003 RUGBY WORLD CUP FINAL: ENGLAND VS. AUSTRALIA

On November 22, 2003, a historic rugby match occurred under the floodlights of a packed Telstra Stadium in Sydney, Australia. The 2003 Rugby World Cup Final between England and Australia featured two of the world's top rugby teams.

Led by the talented Jonny Wilkinson, England faced some tough challenges to reach the finals. Wilkinson was a crucial player in the English team, with his precision and composure instrumental in their success.

Australia, the defending champions, were equally formidable. Under the leadership of their captain, George Gregan, the Wallabies boasted a star-studded lineup. Their backline featured the likes of Mat Rogers, Stirling Mortlock, and Lote Tuqiri, while Nathan Sharpe and George Smith anchored their pack.

The final was thrilling, with both teams exchanging penalties in the first half. England took the lead in the second half, with Jason Robinson scoring a try. However, Australia fought back and scored two tries of their own to level the score.

As the clock ticked towards extra time, the tension was unbearable. In the dying moments of spare time, Jonny Wilkinson scored the most iconic drop goal in rugby history, securing England's victory and crowning them the 2003 Rugby World Cup champions.

This victory was a historic moment for English rugby. It was the first time England had won the Rugby World Cup, and the match was the highest-scoring Rugby World Cup Final of all time. Jonny Wilkinson was named the Man of the Match for his outstanding performance.

The 2003 Rugby World Cup Final will be remembered for generations to come. The story of triumph, courage, and determination inspires young rugby players everywhere to dream big and chase their goals.

England celebrations after winning Rugby World Cup in 2003.

Attribution: By Michael Righi - originally posted to Flickr as Pavel Datsyuk, CC BY-SA 2.0, https://commons.wikimedia.org/w/index.php?curid=4185459

THE 'INVINCIBLE' TOUR OF THE BRITISH AND IRISH LIONS

On May 11, 1974, the British and Irish Lions began their rugby tour of South Africa. They were a team of the best players from England, Scotland, Ireland, and Wales, led by Willie John McBride. Their goal was to make a lasting impression on the rugby world, and they did just that.

Throughout their 22-match tour, the Lions played with skill, camaraderie, and a strong desire to prove themselves. They faced many challenges but grew more confident with each one. The forwards, including Fran Cotton and Fergus Slattery, fought fiercely in the scrums, while the backs, led by Phil Bennett, amazed with their speed and flair.

In the second Test match in Pretoria, the Lions faced the Springboks in thin air, where the conditions were difficult. Despite this, the Lions played with unwavering resolve, resulting in a draw, 12-12. This match was a defining moment of their tour, as they showcased their skill and determination.

Throughout the tour, the Lions remained unbeaten in every match, winning 21 out of 22. Their remarkable achievement was a testament to their skill, resilience, and belief in one another. They became known as 'The Invincibles,' their journey continues to inspire rugby fans of all ages.

The 1974 British and Irish Lions tour of South Africa is a story of greatness, teamwork, and the power of the human spirit. It reminds us that skill, determination, and unity can overcome even the most formidable challenges.

As you step onto the rugby fields, remember 'The Invincible' Tour, and let it inspire you to face challenges head-on, support one another, and play with heart. Rugby is a game of magic and excitement, waiting for the next generation of players to create legendary tales.

A legendary rugby journey began on May 11, 1974, under the South African sun. The British and Irish Lions, a formidable team comprising the best players from England, Scotland, Ireland, and Wales, embarked on a 22-match tour, determined to leave an indelible mark on the rugby world.

Led by the indomitable Willie John McBride, the Lions played with skill, camaraderie, and a burning desire to prove themselves. They faced adversity at every turn, but they grew more assertive with each challenge. The forwards, like Fran Cotton and Fergus Slattery, engaged in fierce battles in the scrums, while the backs, orchestrated by the brilliant fly-half Phil Bennett, dazzled with their speed and flair.

One of the defining moments of this epic journey occurred during the second Test match in Pretoria. In the thin air, where mere mortals struggled to breathe, the Lions faced the Springboks with unwavering resolve. The match ended in a nail-biting draw, 12-12, but the Lions had showcased a level of skill and determination that etched their names in rugby history.

The Lions triumphed over provincial sides, battled through injuries, and formed an unbreakable bond. Every victory, every hard-fought draw, became a testament to the spirit of rugby—the spirit that transcends borders, uniting players from different nations under one common goal.

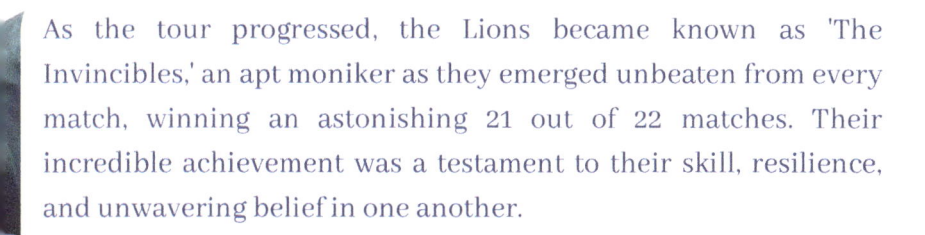

As the tour progressed, the Lions became known as 'The Invincibles,' an apt moniker as they emerged unbeaten from every match, winning an astonishing 21 out of 22 matches. Their incredible achievement was a testament to their skill, resilience, and unwavering belief in one another.

The 1974 British and Irish Lions tour of South Africa is a story that continues to inspire rugby fans of all ages. It is a story about greatness, teamwork, and the power of the human spirit. The Lions' journey reminds us that even the most formidable challenges can be conquered with skill, determination, and unity.

So, my young friends, remember' The Invincible' Tour as you lace up your boots and step onto these hallowed rugby fields. Let it be a beacon of inspiration, a reminder that greatness is achieved not just by winning but by facing challenges head-on, supporting one another, and playing with heart.

The magic of rugby lives on, waiting for the next generation of enthusiasts to create their legendary tales. Embrace the spirit, play with passion, and the next unforgettable story is yours to tell.

British and Irish Lions

THE 1973 BARBARIANS VS. ALL BLACKS MATCH: A TRY FOR THE AGES

Welcome, young rugby enthusiasts! Let me take you back to 1973 when two of the most celebrated rugby teams faced off in Cardiff Arms Park. The All Blacks from New Zealand, who had an unbeaten record of 36 matches, were up against the Barbarians, a daring team known for their free-flowing style of play.

The match was a spectacle from the start. The Barbarians played with flair and spontaneity. The All Blacks were a formidable opponent with their mighty haka and aura of invincibility. But, a moment in the second half elevated this match to rugby folklore.

The ball found its way into the hands of Welsh scrum-half Gareth Edwards, the heartbeat of the Barbarians. What followed was pure magic - a breathtaking sequence of seven passes, weaving through the All Blacks defense effortlessly.

The ball exchanged hands like notes in a symphony, creating a crescendo of anticipation. As the ball reached the hands of the legendary French fullback, Jean-Pierre Rives, he unleashed a burst of speed, dancing past defenders, and then, with sublime grace, offloaded to the flying Fijian, Phil Bennett.

With a sidestep that would make a gazelle envious, Bennett carved through the last line of defense.

The try line beckoned, and in a moment of sheer poetry, Bennett passed inside to the supporting Welshman, JPR Williams, who surged over the line to score a try for the ages.

The crowd erupted, and even the mighty All Blacks couldn't help but applaud. This try wasn't just about points on the board; it was a masterpiece, a symphony of skill, teamwork, and audacity.

The Barbarians emerged victorious, ending the All Blacks' winning streak, but it was more than just a victory. The spirit of camaraderie, the daring creativity, and how they played left an indelible mark on the rugby world.

The 1973 Barbarians versus All Blacks match is a reminder that rugby is not just a game but an art form. Push boundaries, create moments of brilliance, and forge bonds with teammates that will last a lifetime.

So, my young friends, as you lace up your boots and step onto the rugby field, let the spirit of that unforgettable night in 1973 be your guide. Play with joy and creativity, and remember, you're not just playing a game; you're creating memories that will be shared around rugby circles for generations. The magic of rugby lives on, waiting for your story to unfold.

The former National Stadium, Cardiff Arms Park, Cardiff, Wales
By UK Payphone Directory, CC BY-SA 2.0.
https://commons.wikimedia.org/w/index.php?curid=3065113

DID YOU KNOW?

Trivia	Details
Longest Rugby Test Match	The longest rugby test match took place on October 30, 2010, lasting 100 minutes. South Africa emerged victorious 22-17 against England.
First Rugby World Cup	The inaugural Rugby World Cup was held in 1987, co-hosted by New Zealand and Australia, featuring 16 participating teams. New Zealand secured the title.
Highest Individual Points in a Test Match	English fly-half Paul Grayson scored 36 points against Canada on March 13, 1999, setting the record for the most individual points in a Test match.
Drop Goal in 11 Seconds	On August 3, 2002, England's fly-half, Charlie Hodgson, set a record for the fastest drop goal in international rugby, taking only 11 seconds against Romania.
Oldest International Rugby Tournament	The Six Nations Championship, originating in 1883 and contested by England, Scotland, Ireland, and Wales, stands as the oldest international rugby tournament.
Most Drop Goals in a World Cup	Jannie de Beer scored five drop goals during the Rugby World Cup in 1999, with remarkable kicks on October 10, 1999, October 22, 1999, and November 6, 1999.
Highest Scoring Rugby Match	On June 15, 1996, Samoa defeated American Samoa 102-0 in the Pacific Tri-Nations tournament, marking the highest-scoring rugby match.
Only Player to Win World Cups in 15s and 7s	Waisale Serevi from Fiji is the only player to have won both the Rugby World Cup (in 15s) in 1997 and the Rugby World Cup Sevens in 1999 and 2005.
Youngest Rugby World Cup Player	Jonah Lomu, the legendary All Black, became the youngest player to compete in a Rugby World Cup on May 25, 1995.
Most Points Scored in a Calendar Year	Dan Carter, the All Black, holds the record for the most points scored in a calendar year, accumulating 277 points in test matches on November 17, 2012.

3. TRIUMPH AND ADVERSITY

- Martin Johnson: From Captaining England to World Cup Glory
- The Calcutta Cup: England vs. Scotland Rivalry
- David Pocock: Rugby's Advocate for Social Change

MARTIN JOHNSON: FROM CAPTAINING ENGLAND TO WORLD CUP GLORY

Hello, young rugby enthusiasts! On this pleasant evening, surrounded by the rugby fields, I want to share a story that will ignite your passion for the game. Tonight, we'll explore the remarkable journey of Martin Johnson, a true legend whose leadership and resilience defined an era of rugby glory.

Martin Johnson was born on March 9, 1970, in Solihull, England. Standing tall at 6 feet 7 inches, he was a towering figure on the rugby field. Martin's journey to rugby greatness began like many of yours, playing on local pitches, where his dedication and skill set him apart. Soon, he played for the Leicester Tigers, a club that became a crucial stepping stone in his illustrious career.

Martin's path was challenging, but he faced them head-on, honing his physical prowess and leadership skills. These qualities would later define him on the global stage.

Fast forward to November 22, 2003, in Sydney, Australia. The Rugby World Cup final was a spectacle, a clash that had the rugby world holding its breath. England, captained by Martin Johnson, faced their arch-rivals, Australia.

The match was deadlocked at 14-14, and then, in the dying moments of extra time, a calm and collected Jonny Wilkinson stepped up to nail the iconic drop goal that secured England's victory. Jonny Wilkinson's calmness and precision as he slotted home the drop goal was a sight to behold, etching Martin Johnson's name in rugby history and crowning England as World Cup champions.

Martin's leadership, both on and off the field, became a shining example for aspiring rugby players. The triumph wasn't just about winning a World Cup; it was about perseverance, teamwork, and the belief that dreams can come true.

So, my young friends, let Martin Johnson's story fuel your passion for the game. Whether on the pitch or cheering from the sidelines, remember that every challenge is an opportunity for triumph. Keep that rugby spirit alive, and let the stories of legends like Martin Johnson inspire you to pursue your rugby dreams with passion and dedication!

Martin Johnson (Left) and Graham Rowntree

By Patrick Khachfe from London, United Kingdom - Johnno and Graham Rowntree, CC BY-SA 2.0, https://commons.wikimedia.org/w/index.php?curid=9691023

THE CALCUTTA CUP: ENGLAND VS. SCOTLAND RIVALRY

Hello, young rugby enthusiasts! Come over here, pick out your favorite rugby jersey, and delve into the captivating story of the legendary Calcutta Cup rivalry between England and Scotland.

The Origins of a Rivalry

Imagine being right beside the rugby fields on a pleasant evening like this, with the air filled with the echoes of victories and players' camaraderie. In this setting, let me take you back to the historic clashes, fierce battles, and unwavering spirit that define the England vs. Scotland rivalry.

It all began in 1871 when England and Scotland faced the first-ever international rugby match. This historic encounter occurred at Raeburn Place in Edinburgh, Scotland, on March 27, 1871. The match ended in a 1-1 draw, setting the stage for a rivalry of over 150 years.

The Birth of the Calcutta Cup

The Calcutta Cup, a trophy crafted from melted-down rupees, was introduced as the prize for the winner of the annual England vs. Scotland match in 1879. The trophy was donated by the Calcutta Rugby Football Club, a club founded by British expatriates in India in 1872. The name "Calcutta Cup" reflects the club's origins and rugby's significance in India during the British Raj.

A Rivalry Steeped in History and Tradition

As the years passed, the competition between England and Scotland intensified. England, with its iconic red rose emblem, and Scotland, proudly displaying the thistle, locked horns in a series of epic encounters.

The matches were not just about winning a cup; they were about national pride, about showcasing the grit and determination that define the heart of rugby.

Scotland's Historic Victory at Twickenham

Fast forward to 1925 - a year that rugby enthusiasts will never forget. Scotland achieved a historic victory over England at Twickenham Stadium in London on February 7, 1925.

This was the first time Scotland had won the Calcutta Cup at Twickenham, and the celebrations were monumental. The spirit of triumph echoed through the Scottish ranks, marking a significant moment in the rivalry.

Scotland's Golden Era and the Rise of Rugby Legends

The 1970s witnessed a golden era for Scottish rugby, and their triumphs over England added glorious chapters to the rivalry. Names like Andy Irvine, Colin Deans, and Gavin Hastings became synonymous with Scottish valor on the rugby field.

These players showcased exceptional talent and contributed to Scotland's dominance during this period.

England's Resurgence and the Continued Rivalry

However, adversity struck again. England, with their own resurgence, demonstrated resilience and skill that kept the rivalry alive and kicking.

England's resurgence showcased the depth and talent within English rugby, ensuring that the rivalry continued to produce thrilling matches.

A Legacy of Triumph and Adversity

On this pleasant evening beside the rugby fields, we pay tribute to the spirit of the England vs. Scotland rivalry - the triumphs that bring joy, the adversities that fuel determination, and the legacy that continues to inspire generations of rugby players.

Lessons from the Calcutta Cup Matches

As you embark on your rugby journey, remember the lessons of the Calcutta Cup matches. It's not just about the final score; it's about the passion, the camaraderie, and the indomitable spirit that make rugby a sport like no other. Embrace the challenges, celebrate the victories, and never lose sight of your love for the game.

Until next time, my young friends, keep that rugby spirit alive, and let the stories of epic rivalries inspire you to create your tales of triumph and adversity on the rugby field!

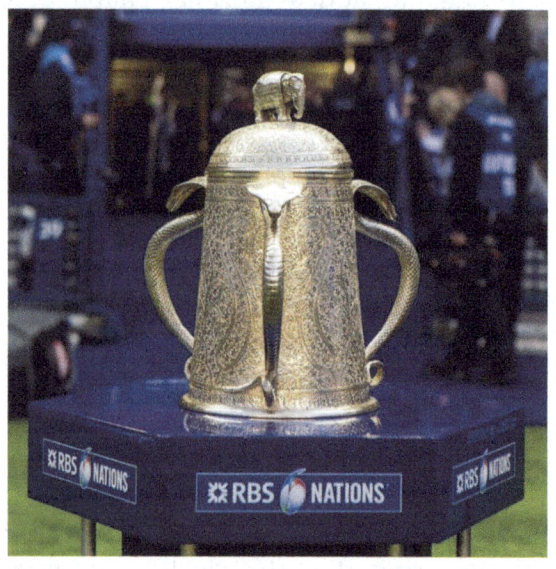

Trophy awarded to the winner of the annual Six Nations Championship
By JaCastro7 - Own work, CC BY-SA 4.0, https://commons.wikimedia.org/w/index.php?curid=69655588

DAVID POCOCK: RUGBY'S ADVOCATE FOR SOCIAL CHANGE

If you're a young rugby enthusiast, gather around and find a comfy spot on the grass. Let me regale you with an extraordinary tale beyond the try lines and tackles. This is the inspiring story of David Pocock, a rugby player whose journey transcends the field's boundaries, making him a true advocate for social change.

David Pocock was born on April 23, 1988, in Gweru, Zimbabwe. Growing up in the African bush, David didn't have a typical rugby upbringing. However, his family moved to Australia when he was a young boy, where his rugby journey truly began. His prowess on the field quickly caught attention, and by the age of 18, he made his Super Rugby debut for the Western Force. But David was not only making strides in rugby but also cultivating a sense of responsibility and empathy that would set him apart.

Fast forward to his international career with the Australian national team, the Wallabies, and David's tenacity, skill, and leadership were evident. However, his off-field actions truly defined him. In an era where athletes are often confined to the role of sports figures, David emerged as a voice for the voiceless.

His advocacy for social and environmental causes became a hallmark of his career. Whether it was campaigning against homophobia in sports, addressing climate change, or standing up for the rights of refugees, David Pocock became a beacon of hope and change. He showed the world that athletes could be more than just players—they could be catalysts for a better, more inclusive world.

David faced his fair share of challenges, from injuries that threatened his rugby career to the criticism that sometimes accompanies those who dare to speak out. Yet, like a true warrior, he pressed on, using his setbacks as stepping stones to greater heights.

As we sit here, surrounded by the echoes of rugby practice and the setting sun, let David Pocock's story inspire us. Let it remind us that our actions, both on and off the field, can shape the world around us. Rugby isn't just a game of tries and tackles; it's a platform for change, and David Pocock exemplifies that spirit.

So, my young friends, as you lace up your boots and step onto the rugby field, remember the tale of David Pocock. Be bold, be compassionate, and, in the face of adversity, be the change you wish to see in the world. Until next time, keep that rugby spirit alive!

David Pocock

By Magee425 - Own work, CC BY-SA 4.0, https://commons.wikimedia.org/w/index.php?curid=118229206

DID YOU KNOW?

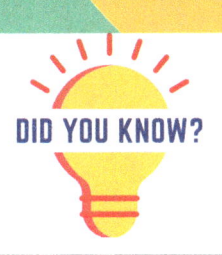

#	Facts
1.	The first international rugby match took place in 1871 between England and Scotland, ending in a 1-1 draw.
2.	The Calcutta Cup, the oldest rugby trophy in the world, was first awarded in 1879 to the winner of the annual England vs. Scotland match.
3.	In 1925, Scotland achieved a historic victory over England, marking the first time they lifted the Calcutta Cup at Twickenham Stadium.
4.	During the 1970s, Scotland witnessed a golden era of rugby, with players like Andy Irvine, Colin Deans, and Gavin Hastings becoming synonymous with Scottish rugby prowess.
5.	The Webb Ellis Cup, the trophy awarded to the winner of the Rugby World Cup, was named after William Webb Ellis, who is credited with catching a football during a school game in 1823, an act that is considered the origin of rugby football.
6.	The haka, the traditional war cry performed by the New Zealand All Blacks rugby team before matches, has its roots in Māori culture and is intended to intimidate opponents and boost the team's spirit.
7.	The Fijian rugby team is known for its flamboyant style of play, incorporating traditional Fijian dances and chants into their pre-match rituals.
8.	The British Lions, a composite team of players from England, Scotland, and Wales, embark on a series of tours every four years, facing the Springboks of South Africa, the Wallabies of Australia, or the All Blacks of New Zealand.
9.	The Rugby World Cup, held every four years since 1987, is the pinnacle of international rugby union competition, with New Zealand currently holding the record for most titles won (3).
10.	Rugby Sevens, a fast-paced, seven-a-side variant of rugby union, made its Olympic debut at the 2016 Rio Games and has quickly gained popularity worldwide.

4. WOMEN IN RUGBY

- Emily Scarratt: England's Star on the Rise
- Black Ferns: Dominance in Women's Rugby
- Respect and Equality: The Progress of Women's Rugby

EMILY SCARRATT: ENGLAND'S STAR ON THE RISE

Welcome, young rugby enthusiasts, to a world where athleticism and determination combine to create a thrilling and inspiring sporting experience. Today, we will journey into the life of Emily Scarratt, England's rising star, and explore her trailblazing achievements that have shattered boundaries and inspired countless young girls.

Emily's love for rugby began in Leicester, England, where she discovered her passion for the sport early. From the moment she stepped onto the field, she was captivated by the game's thrill, her teammates' camaraderie, and the contest's physicality. Rugby became her sanctuary, where she could unleash her boundless energy and unwavering spirit.

As Emily progressed through the ranks, her talent flourished. Her speed was electrifying, her agility mesmerizing, and her determination unyielding. She possessed a remarkable ability to weave through defenders like a phantom, leaving them in her wake. Her powerful kicks could send the ball soaring through the air, instilling fear in the hearts of her opponents.

However, Emily's impact extended far beyond the field. She inspired young girls, proving that rugby was not just a man's sport. She shattered stereotypes and demonstrated that women could be fierce, determined, and thrive in this demanding sport. Emily's dedication to rugby was unwavering.

She trained relentlessly, pushing her body to the limit and never relinquishing her dreams.

She faced obstacles and setbacks along the way, but she never wavered. Instead, she used these challenges to fuel her determination, emerging even more resolute in her pursuit of greatness.

Her efforts paid off spectacularly. Emily's meteoric rise to stardom propelled her into the heart of the England women's rugby team. She represented her country with unwavering pride and passion, becoming a cornerstone of their numerous victories. Her impact on the team was undeniable, and her name became synonymous with rugby excellence.

In 2014, Emily was instrumental in guiding England to victory in the Rugby World Cup, a crowning achievement that cemented her legacy as one of the game's greatest icons. Her performance in the final was extraordinary as she scored a crucial try and converted a penalty that secured England's triumph in the dying moments of the match.

Emily's achievements extend beyond the Rugby World Cup. She has been a driving force behind England's dominance in the Six Nations Championship, securing multiple Grand Slams and earning the coveted Player of the Championship award on numerous occasions. In 2019, she was bestowed with the prestigious World Rugby Women's 15s Player of the Year award, a testament to her exceptional talent and unwavering dedication to the sport.

Emily Scarratt is more than just a rugby player; she symbolizes resilience, determination, and passion.

Her journey is a testament to the power of dreams and the belief in one's abilities. She has inspired countless young girls to pursue their rugby aspirations and paved the way for a future where gender is no longer a defining factor in pursuing sporting excellence.

So, as you embark on your rugby journey, let Emily's story be your guiding light. Let her unwavering spirit ignite your passion, and let her determination fuel your dreams. Remember, with hard work, dedication, and belief in yourselves, you can achieve greatness in rugby and beyond.

Emily Scarratt

By Pierre-Yves Beaudouin / Wikimedia Commons, CC BY-SA 4.0, https://commons.wikimedia.org/w/index.php?curid=36004969

BLACK FERNS: DOMINANCE IN WOMEN'S RUGBY

Hello, young rugby enthusiasts! Let me take you on a journey to the world of the Black Ferns, a team that has made a significant impact on women's rugby. They have redefined dominance in the sport through their passion, determination, and pursuit of excellence.

Imagine yourself in a stadium on a warm summer evening, surrounded by the camaraderie of friends, and the excitement of a rugby match. Now, let me transport you to the heart of the Black Ferns' legacy. A place where their perseverance, skill, and unwavering commitment to excellence have taken them beyond the try lines.

The Black Ferns originated from New Zealand, where they have made a name for themselves as pioneers of women's rugby. These strong women, dressed in black jerseys, have shattered preconceived notions about women in sports and conquered their opponents.

Their journey is a testament to the resilience of the human spirit. The Black Ferns have faced challenges head-on and broke through barriers that once seemed impossible. Their passion for rugby inspired young girls worldwide to dream without limits.

One of the most remarkable moments in the history of the Black Ferns is the Rugby World Cup final, where they demonstrated their mastery of the sport. They showed unmatched skill, teamwork, and unwavering determination.

Their performance was not only a victory but a symphony of triumph, resonating with the echoes of hard work and dedication. The Black Ferns embody the spirit of rugby - a game that brings people together and transcends borders.

These athletes are ambassadors off the field, encouraging the next generation of rugby enthusiasts to pursue their passion with grit and grace. Their unwavering commitment to each other and the sport makes them truly remarkable.

Let the story of the Black Ferns inspire you to push your limits, embrace challenges with open arms, and foster a love for rugby beyond the game itself. Whether you are an aspiring player or a supporter, the Black Ferns' journey teaches us that you can achieve greatness with determination, camaraderie, and unwavering belief in yourself.

Here are some fascinating facts and trivia about the Black Ferns to add to your knowledge and inspire your rugby journey:

- The Black Ferns are the most successful women's rugby team in history, having won five Rugby World Cups, more than any other nation.

- They have an incredible winning record of over 90%, a testament to their consistent dominance and unparalleled skill.

- The Black Ferns hold the record for the most consecutive wins in women's international rugby, with 56 victories.

- The iconic black jersey worn by the Black Ferns is considered one of the most recognizable and respected symbols in women's sports.

- The Black Ferns have inspired countless young girls to pursue their rugby dreams, breaking down barriers and paving the way for a more inclusive and equitable sporting landscape.

So, my young friends, let the Black Ferns' legacy be a beacon of inspiration on your rugby journeys. As you dream of victories and strive for excellence, may the spirit of these extraordinary women fuel your passion for the game. The rugby field awaits, and who knows, perhaps one day we'll share stories of your triumphs inspired by the indomitable spirit of the Black Ferns.

Black Ferns

By Pierre-Yves Beaudouin / Wikimedia Commons, CC BY-SA 4.0, https://commons.wikimedia.org/w/index.php?curid=36004969

RESPECT AND EQUALITY: THE PROGRESS OF WOMEN'S RUGBY

Welcome, young rugby enthusiasts, to a captivating journey through time as we witness the remarkable progress of women's rugby. This story is about respect, equality, and the unstoppable spirit of change.

Imagine a lovely evening beside the rugby fields, where the echoes of laughter and the excitement of the game fill the air. Now, picture the rugby fields of the past, where the crowd's roar was often reserved for the men on the pitch. But fear not, for this story is about the seismic shift that transformed the landscape of women's rugby.

A few decades ago, women playing rugby at the highest level seemed like a distant dream. Women were often discouraged or even banned from participating in the sport, considered too physical and demanding for their "delicate" frames.

But dreams have a way of evolving into reality, and this story is a testament to the tireless efforts of countless women who dared to challenge the status quo. These courageous women faced skepticism and resistance, but their love for the game and unwavering determination propelled them forward.

Did you know that the first official women's rugby match took place in England in 1884?

Despite facing opposition from authorities and fellow athletes, these pioneering women defied expectations and demonstrated their passion for the sport.

Their perseverance gradually led to a more formal structure for women's rugby, paving the way for future generations of players.

In the late 19th and early 20th centuries, women's rugby continued to grow in popularity, with informal matches being organized across the globe. These matches often defied social norms, showcasing women athletes' skill, strength, and resilience.

A significant turning point came in 1978 when the International Rugby Board (IRB), now World Rugby, officially recognized women's rugby. This recognition opened the doors for international competition, establishing the first Women's Rugby World Cup in 1991.

The inaugural Women's Rugby World Cup, held in Wales, was momentous, bringing together teams from 12 nations. The tournament was a resounding success, highlighting the growing talent and competitiveness of women's rugby on a global scale.

Since then, women's rugby has flourished, attracting players from over 100 countries and becoming increasingly professionalized. Top players now earn full-time salaries and compete in high-profile tournaments, demonstrating the sport's growing recognition and appeal.

Today, women's rugby is a global phenomenon, with teams from all corners showcasing their skill, strength, and passion for the game. The Rugby World Cup has become a significant event in the sporting calendar, attracting millions of viewers worldwide and inspiring countless young girls to pursue their rugby dreams.

The story of women's rugby is a testament to the power of determination, the unwavering pursuit of equality, and the transformative spirit of sport. These remarkable women have shattered stereotypes, challenged perceptions, and paved the way for future generations of rugby enthusiasts.

As the sun dips below the horizon on this rugby field, remember the journey of these trailblazers. Let their stories be a reminder that progress is not always swift, but with perseverance and a love for the game, barriers can be shattered, and dreams can take flight.

So, whether you're a player, a supporter, or a dreamer, know that the rugby field is a space for everyone. Let the progress of women's rugby inspire you to challenge expectations, embrace diversity, and champion respect and equality. The future of rugby is bright, and each of you has a role in this evolving story. As you stand on the sidelines or charge onto the pitch, remember the journey of those who came before you, and let their legacy fuel your passion for the game.

DID YOU KNOW?

Year	Event	Details
1884	First Women's Rugby Match	The first official women's rugby match occurred in Handsworth, England, on March 27, 1884. Rochdale Hornets won over Cleckheaton Ladies' Rugby Club by 2 goals and 1 try to nil. Despite facing opposition, these pioneering women defied expectations, showcasing their passion for the sport.
1978	Recognition by International Rugby Board (IRB)	Women's rugby gained official recognition by the International Rugby Board (now World Rugby) in 1978. This recognition paved the way for international competition and led to the establishment of the first Women's Rugby World Cup in 1991. It marked a significant milestone, providing legitimacy, funding, and opportunities for female players.
1991	Inaugural Women's Rugby World Cup	The first Women's Rugby World Cup was held in Wales in 1991, bringing together teams from 12 nations. The United States emerged victorious, defeating the host nation Wales in a thrilling final, showcasing the growing talent and competitiveness of women's rugby on a global scale.
Every 4 Years	Women's Rugby World Cup	Since its inception in 1991, the Women's Rugby World Cup has been held every four years. New Zealand, represented by the Black Ferns, has dominated the tournament, winning the most titles (five) and showcasing incredible skill, teamwork, and determination, highlighting the remarkable achievements of women's rugby.
Ongoing	Professionalization of Women's Rugby	Women's rugby has become increasingly professionalized, with top players earning full-time salaries and participating in high-profile tournaments such as the Women's Six Nations Championship and the Women's Super Rugby League. This professionalization has elevated the quality of play and raised the profile of women's rugby, attracting more fans and sponsors.
2022	Global Female Rugby Players Estimate	In 2022, World Rugby estimated that there were over 2.7 million registered female rugby players globally. This growth is attributed to increased visibility, more opportunities for girls to participate, and a growing recognition of women's athletic capabilities in rugby.
Ongoing	Women's Rugby in the Sporting Calendar	Women's rugby has become a major event in the sporting calendar, attracting millions of viewers worldwide. Tournaments like the Rugby World Cup inspire countless young girls to pursue their rugby dreams, contributing to the growing popularity of women's rugby and capturing the attention of fans and media alike.
Ongoing	Breaking Gender Stereotypes and Promoting Inclusivity	Women's rugby has played a crucial role in breaking down gender stereotypes and promoting inclusivity in sports. The sport showcases that women can excel in physically demanding, traditionally male-dominated sports, challenging stereotypes and creating new pathways for women in sports.
Ongoing	Characteristics of Women's Rugby	Women's rugby is a dynamic and exciting sport that showcases teamwork, skill, and athleticism. The game's unique blend of physicality, strategy, and camaraderie appeals to players of all ages and backgrounds. The fast-paced nature, unpredictable twists, and displays of individual brilliance keep spectators on the edge of their seats.
Ongoing	Bright Future for Women's Rugby	The future of women's rugby is bright, with continued growth, professionalization, and global exposure. The sport has the potential to inspire generations of young girls to embrace their passion for rugby and pursue their dreams on the field. The world eagerly anticipates the incredible achievements that lie ahead in women's rugby.

5. UNDERDOG STORIES

- Japan's Historic Upset: Rugby World Cup 2015
- The 'Swing Low, Sweet Chariot' England Anthem
- The Legacy of Richie McCaw: A Rugby Hero

JAPAN'S HISTORIC UPSET: RUGBY WORLD CUP 2015

Gather around, young rugby enthusiasts! Let us embark on a captivating journey into one of the most inspirational underdog stories in the annals of rugby: Japan's historic upset at the Rugby World Cup in 2015.

Imagine a pleasant evening by the rugby fields, filled with the exhilarating sounds of the game and the palpable excitement of what's to come. Now, let your imagination transport you to England in 2015, where the Rugby World Cup was set to unfold, and a team from the Land of the Rising Sun was about to make history.

Our tale begins with the Japan national rugby team, often considered the underdogs in rugby. On September 19, 2015, they stepped onto the hallowed turf of Brighton's Community Stadium to face the mighty South Africa in their opening match. Not many expected the seismic shift that was about to occur.

South Africa was a formidable opponent, a two-time Rugby World Cup champion, and a powerhouse in world rugby. The odds were stacked against Japan, ranked 13th in the world then, while the Springboks were ranked third. However, the beauty of rugby lies in its unpredictability, and that fateful day would prove to be a testament to the indomitable spirit of determination and unwavering belief.

As the match unfolded, the underdog Japanese team showcased tenacity, skill, and tactical brilliance, leaving spectators in awe. The intensity on the field was palpable, and it became clear that this was no ordinary contest.

The defining moment came in the dying minutes of the game. Japan, against all odds, found themselves trailing by a single point. The tension was electric, and the rugby world held its breath. Then, like a scene from a storybook, Japan executed a series of brilliant passes and strategic moves that culminated in a dramatic try by Karne Hesketh in the 80th minute, securing an astonishing victory.

The final score: Japan 34, South Africa 32. The rugby world was left in disbelief, and Japan had not only won a match but had delivered a historic upset that reverberated across the globe. The victory sent shockwaves through the sporting world, as it was the first time a Tier 3 nation had defeated a Tier 1 nation in a Rugby World Cup pool match.

What made this underdog story genuinely inspiring was the win and the spirit with which it was achieved. The Japanese team, led by coach Eddie Jones, exemplified rugby's core values: teamwork, resilience, and the belief that anything is possible with dedication and heart.

Remember the tale of Japan's historic upset as the sun sets on this rugby field. Let it be a reminder that in rugby, as in life, the underdogs can triumph over the giants. No matter the odds stacked against you, believe in your abilities and the unwavering support of your teammates, as it can lead to incredible victories.

So, young friends, as you lace up your boots and step onto the rugby field, channel the spirit of Japan's remarkable journey. Let it inspire you to dream big, work hard, and embrace the joy of the game.

In rugby, underdog stories are often the most magical, and who knows, one day, we might be telling tales of your triumphs under the evening sky beside these rugby fields.

THE 'SWING LOW, SWEET CHARIOT' ENGLAND ANTHEM

Young rugby enthusiasts, gather around and let me tell you a story that blends the magic of rugby with the powerful anthem "Swing Low, Sweet Chariot," which played a significant role in England's historic upset during the 1988 Rugby match against Ireland.

Imagine a warm evening beside Twickenham's iconic rugby fields, where the air is filled with camaraderie. The England team, often considered underdogs, faced a formidable Ireland.

Tensions were high, and every play held the crowd breathless. The stadium, known as 'The Rugby Cathedral,' echoed with the passion of its fans.

48

In 1988, amid this electric atmosphere, England supporters spontaneously started singing "Swing Low, Sweet Chariot." The melody, steeped in history, spread like wildfire, capturing the spirit of unity. The players on the pitch drew strength from the chorus, and England, fueled by the powerful synergy of rugby and song, staged a remarkable comeback.

Against all odds, the underdogs secured a historic victory with the final score: England 34, Ireland 32. "Swing Low, Sweet Chariot" became an anthem, etching its place in rugby folklore, symbolizing triumph, unity, and the joy of being part of the rugby family.

Stand beside these rugby fields on a pleasant evening and let the power of "Swing Low, Sweet Chariot" echo through the stands. Let it inspire you to celebrate the game and the shared experience of being part of something greater than yourself – a community bound by a love for rugby and the joy of supporting your team.

So, my young friends, let the anthem be your soundtrack on your rugby journey. Whether you're cheering from the stands, laces tied, ready to charge down the field, or reveling in the camaraderie of fellow rugby enthusiasts, remember the magic of "Swing Low, Sweet Chariot." It's a song that celebrates the underdog, the triumph of unity, and the pure joy of being part of the rugby family. Who knows, perhaps one day you'll be part of a story that resonates just as sweetly beside these rugby fields.

Now, let's look at that historic 1988 Rugby match. Wearing their iconic white jerseys, the England team found themselves trailing against Ireland. Every pass, tackle, and try was a heartbeat in the game's narrative.

It was a fierce battle where the underdogs faced adversity, but the spirit of "Swing Low, Sweet Chariot" echoing through Twickenham catalyzed a monumental comeback.

England turned the tide as the match progressed, fueled by the anthem's energy. The players, inspired by the resounding chorus from the stands, showcased unwavering determination. The stadium roared as England secured the victory with a final score 34 to Ireland's 32.

This match wasn't just about rugby; it was a testament to the synergy of sport and spirit, where a song symbolized triumph. The connection between "Swing Low, Sweet Chariot" and victory remains etched in rugby history, reminding us all that, in rugby, even the underdogs can achieve the extraordinary.

Twickenham Stadium

By https://www.flickr.com/photos/t_abdelmoumen Tijani59 - https://www.flickr.com/photos/t_abdelmoumen/3402592224/, CC BY-SA 2.0, https://commons.wikimedia.org/w/index.php?curid=6447170

Traditional white England shirt

By https://www.flickr.com/photos/t_abdelmoumen Tijani59 - https://www.flickr.com/photos/t_abdelmoumen/3402592224/, CC BY-SA 2.0, https://commons.wikimedia.org/w/index.php?curid=6447170

50

THE LEGACY OF RICHIE MCCAW: A RUGBY HERO

Young rugby enthusiasts gather around as the sun sets and shadows stretch across these fields. I want to tell you about the underdog who became a rugby hero - Richie McCaw.

Imagine a young boy named Richie McCaw growing up in the small town of Kurow, New Zealand, surrounded by the grandeur of the Southern Alps. From the moment he first laced up his rugby boots, he was captivated by the game's intensity, the thrill of the chase, and the camaraderie formed with teammates on the field.

Richie faced challenges because he wasn't the biggest or the strongest, but his unyielding spirit and hunger for improvement set him apart. With each setback, he dusted himself off, embraced the lessons rugby taught him and emerged stronger.

As Richie climbed the ranks, his tenacity became a beacon of inspiration. His work ethic was unmatched, and his commitment to the game was unwavering. Despite the skeptics who doubted his ability to lead, Richie wore his underdog status as a badge of honor, proving that size and strength are not the only measures of a proper rugby hero.

The turning point came when Richie earned the coveted All Blacks jersey, leading the national team with humility and an unassuming demeanor that endeared him to teammates and fans alike. Under Richie's captaincy, the All Blacks achieved unprecedented success, winning the Rugby World Cup twice, in 2011 and 2015, and securing a record-breaking 18 consecutive Test wins, showcasing their dominance on the global stage.

Richie McCaw symbolized perseverance and leadership on and off the field. His calm under pressure, ability to inspire his teammates, and unwavering commitment to excellence made him a role model for aspiring rugby players worldwide.

Richie faced injuries, defeats, and personal sacrifices with stoic resolve, leaving an indelible mark on the sport. He never made excuses, always striving for self-improvement and pushing his teammates to do the same.

Richie McCaw's achievements are remarkable. He is the most capped Test player in rugby history, with 148 appearances for New Zealand. He captained the All Blacks to two Rugby World Cup victories and led them to a record-breaking 18 consecutive Test wins. His leadership and skills earned him the World Rugby Player of the Year award three times, and he was named New Zealand Sportsman of the Year twice.

Envision Richie McCaw, a rugby hero who emerged from the shadows of doubt to etch his legacy in the very fabric of rugby history. His story is a testament to the belief that no matter where you come from or the obstacles in your path, you can rise above and achieve greatness with determination, resilience, and a love for the game.

So, remember that every tackle, every sprint, every triumph is a part of your unique story. The underdog can become the hero; in rugby, the journey is just as important as the destination. Never underestimate your potential, and always strive to be the best version of yourself, both on and off the field.

Richie McCaw

By New Zealand Government, Office of the Governor-General - https://gg.govt.nz/file/13589, CC BY 4.0, https://commons.wikimedia.org/w/index.php?curid=89462549

Richie McCaw Record	Achievement
Most capped Test player in rugby history	148 appearances for New Zealand
Rugby World Cup wins as captain	2 (2011 and 2015)
Record-breaking consecutive Test wins	18
World Rugby Player of the Year awards	3 (2006, 2009, and 2010)
Halberg Award for New Zealand Sportsman of the Year	2 (2010 and 2011)

DID YOU KNOW?

Underdog Stories	Interesting Facts and Trivia
Japan's Historic Upset: Rugby World Cup 2015	1. Brave Blossoms: Japan's national rugby team is nicknamed the "Brave Blossoms."
	2. David vs. Goliath: In the 2015 Rugby World Cup, Japan, ranked 13th, upset two-time world champions South Africa.
	3. Last-Minute Triumph: Karne Hesketh's last-minute try secured Japan's historic 34-32 victory against South Africa.
	4. Eddie Jones: The coach behind Japan's triumph, Eddie Jones, later became the head coach of England, leading them to the 2019 Rugby World Cup final.
The 'Swing Low, Sweet Chariot' England Anthem	5. Spontaneous Anthem: Fans began singing "Swing Low, Sweet Chariot" spontaneously during a 1988 match against Ireland, turning it into a cherished tradition.
	6. Historical Roots: The anthem has historical roots as an African-American spiritual song, expressing hope for freedom from slavery.
	7. Rugby and Song Unite: The anthem's association with England's rugby team exemplifies how a song can become a powerful rallying cry for players and fans.
The Legacy of Richie McCaw: A Rugby Hero	8. Kurow's Pride: Richie McCaw hails from Kurow, a small New Zealand town, showcasing rugby's universal appeal.
	9. All Blacks Captaincy: McCaw captained the All Blacks for a record 110 test matches, leading them to numerous victories, including two Rugby World Cup titles.
	10. Exceptional Work Ethic: McCaw's dedication to constant improvement and resilience in the face of challenges set him apart as a true rugby hero.

6. YOUNG RUGBY HEROES

- Billy Vunipola: A Rising Star in English Rugby
- James O'Connor: From Young Sensation to Redemption
- The Future Stars: Aspiring Young Rugby Talents

BILLY VUNIPOLA: A RISING STAR IN ENGLISH RUGBY

Gather 'round, young rugby enthusiasts, as the sun paints a warm glow across these rugby fields. In this story, we'll explore the inspiring journey of Billy Vunipola, a rising star in English rugby.

Billy, a lad with roots tracing back to Tonga, a tiny island in the Pacific, had a strong passion for the game since his early rugby days. Despite facing challenges in a new country, his love for the sport never faded. Billy brought down a larger opponent in a fearless charge in one memorable school match, showcasing his never-say-die spirit.

From local clubs to the prestigious Saracens, Billy's rise to success was like a shooting star across the rugby sky. His powerful runs and ability to bulldoze through defenders left a trail of inspiration for young players. But it wasn't just his on-field performance that made him a rugby icon; his off-pitch spirit was equally captivating. He was humble, genuine, and respectful and embodied rugby's brotherhood and community values.

As he donned the English jersey with pride, Billy's determination endeared him to rugby enthusiasts worldwide. He was known for his 'Billy Bonus' celebration, a playful dance move after scoring, reflecting his infectious personality and connection with the crowd.

Beyond rugby, Billy was also a talented musician, playing the guitar and singing. This creative side demonstrated his well-rounded personality. During the 2015 Rugby World Cup, his unwavering determination inspired England to a crucial victory, and he was a vocal advocate for diversity and inclusion in rugby.

Some of Billy Vunipola's significant accomplishments include making his debut for Saracens in 2013, winning Premiership Player of the Year in 2014, winning European Player of the Year in 2016, being selected for the British & and Irish Lions three times, and playing a pivotal role in England's victory in the 2015 Rugby World Cup.

Billy Vunipola is more than just a rugby hero; he's a role model for facing life's challenges. His story teaches us that dreams can take flight with hard work, determination, and a positive attitude. So, whether you're charging down the field, tackling challenges, or reveling in the joy of the game, remember every rugby hero started as a young enthusiast with a love for the sport. One day, your story will echo sweetly across these rugby fields.

Here are some of Billy Vunipola's significant accomplishments:
- He made his debut for Saracens in 2013
- Won Premiership Player of the Year in 2014
- Won European Player of the Year in 2016
- Selected for the British & and Irish Lions three times
- Played a crucial role in England's victory in the 2015 Rugby World Cup

Vunipola is a true rugby hero, and his story is an inspiration to young people around the world.

Billy Vunipola

By Clément Bucco-Lechat - Own work, CC BY-SA 3.0, https://commons.wikimedia.org/w/index.php?curid=46847548

JAMES O'CONNOR: FROM YOUNG SENSATION TO REDEMPTION

Gather around, young rugby enthusiasts, as the sun casts a warm glow across these hallowed fields. Let me take you on a journey to the world of rugby, where a young star named James O'Connor illuminated the game with his undeniable talent and unwavering spirit.

Picture this: a warm evening beside the iconic Suncorp Stadium in Brisbane, Australia. The air is excited, and the crowd's roar echoes through the stands. It's in this electrifying atmosphere that James O'Connor's story unfolds - a tale of raw talent, unwavering determination, and the belief that dreams can come true.

James O'Connor was born on the Gold Coast of Australia in 1990, and his rugby journey began at five. With a rugby ball in hand, he spent countless hours honing his skills, and his passion for the game grew with each passing day. At the age of 11, James moved to Auckland, New Zealand, with his family, and it was here that his rugby dreams began to take flight.

James's raw talent was evident from the beginning. He possessed a unique blend of power, speed, and an innate understanding of the game. His ability to break tackles, score tries, and orchestrate his team's attacks made him a force to be reckoned with on the pitch.

<u>Trivia Fact 1</u>: James O'Connor holds the record for the youngest player ever to score a try for the Wallabies, achieving this feat at 18.

James O'Connor

By Salman Javed - Flickr: Wales vs Australia, CC BY-SA 2.0.
https://commons.wikimedia.org/w/index.php?curid=17129713

As James progressed through the ranks, his reputation as a rising star grew. He captained Queensland's under-18 and under-20 teams, leading them to victories in the Australian Rugby Championship and Junior World Cup competitions. His performances caught the attention of the Queensland Reds, one of Australia's top rugby clubs, and in 2008, at 18, James made his professional debut.

<u>Trivia Fact 2</u>: James O'Connor is one of only a few players to have won the John Eales Medal twice, receiving this prestigious award in 2011 and 2013.

James's impact was immediate. His powerful runs, deft passing skills, and ability to read the game made him an invaluable asset to the Reds team. He played a pivotal role in their Super Rugby and Currie Cup victories, earning him the prestigious title of John Eales Medalist in 2011.

<u>Trivia Fact 3</u>: James O'Connor has the unique distinction of having played for Australia and England, representing the Wallabies from 2008 to 2013 and then the English national team in 2016.

James's meteoric rise continued with his selection for the Australian national team, the Wallabies, in 2008. He quickly established himself as a key player, his performances marked by his trademark power, tenacity, and ability to inspire his teammates. In 2011, James was a key member of the Wallabies team that reached the Rugby World Cup final, showcasing his talent on the global stage.

Trivia Fact 4: James O'Connor is known for his incredible versatility, having played in various positions throughout his career, including fly-half, center, and fullback.

But James O'Connor's story is not just about his on-field achievements but also his character and unwavering determination. Despite facing injuries and setbacks, James has always bounced back more muscular, his resolve never wavering.

He inspires young rugby players worldwide, demonstrating that anything is possible with hard work, dedication, and a love for the game.

Trivia Fact 5: James O'Connor is a passionate advocate for mental health awareness, using his platform to encourage others to seek help if they are struggling.

In 2013, James made the difficult decision to leave Australia to pursue opportunities in Europe. He spent several years playing for Toulon and London Irish, where he continued to develop as a player and mature as a person.

In 2019, James returned triumphantly to the Wallabies, again donning the green and gold jersey. His comeback was a testament to his resilience and unwavering commitment to the game he loved.

James played a key role in the Wallabies' campaign at the Rugby World Cup that year, demonstrating that he was still one of the best players in the world.

James O'Connor's story is one of redemption, growth, and the unyielding spirit of a young rugby hero. He has faced adversity and emerged stronger, proving that setbacks are not the end but the beginning of a new chapter. His journey teaches us that we can achieve anything we set our minds to with hard work, determination, and a love for the game

THE FUTURE STARS: ASPIRING YOUNG RUGBY TALENTS

Gather around, young rugby enthusiasts, as the twilight paints the sky in hues of orange and purple, and let the spirit of rugby fill the air. Tonight, we embark on a journey into the world of aspiring young rugby talents, the future stars who are weaving their dreams amidst these hallowed fields.

Beneath the fading light, imagine a group of youngsters with stars in their eyes chasing the oval ball with infectious energy and dreams of emulating their rugby heroes. Their laughter echoes through the air, their passion radiating like the setting sun, casting their dreams into the twilight sky.

Let me introduce you to some up-and-coming rugby players already making waves on the international stage.

Will Jordan (New Zealand)
Will Jordan is a 23-year-old wing for the New Zealand All Blacks. He was named World Rugby Breakthrough Player of the Year in 2021 and the top try-scorer at the Rugby World Cup in 2023. He is known for his electrifying pace, aerial prowess, and ability to score tries from anywhere on the field.

Carter Gordon (Australia)
Carter Gordon is a 22-year-old fly-half for the Australian Wallabies. He was named Super Rugby Rookie of the Year in 2022 and made his Wallabies debut at the age of 20. He started all five games for Australia at Rugby World Cup 2023 and is known for his composure and leadership qualities.

Will Jordan    Carter Gordon

Damian Penaud (France)

Damian Penaud is a 24-year-old wing for the French Les Bleus. He was the Top 14 Try Scorer for the 2022-23 season and a member of the France Six Nations Championship 2023 winning squad. He is known for his mesmerizing footwork, evasive running, and ability to create scoring opportunities.

Louis Bielle-Biarrey (France)

Louis Bielle-Biarrey is a 22-year-old prop for the French Les Bleus. He was a member of the Espoirs Championship 2022 winning team and made his Top 14 debut at 19. He started all seven games for France at the Rugby World Cup in 2023 and is known for his power, technique, and work ethic.

Damian Penaud

By Société Générale - https://www.youtube.com/watch?v=LVq_xr-L3gw, CC BY 3.0, https://commons.wikimedia.org/w/index.php?curid=129542984

Louis Bielle-Biarrey

By JohnNewton8 - Own work, CC BY-SA 4.0, https://commons.wikimedia.org/w/index.php?curid=122322841

Juan Martin Gonzalez (Argentina)

Juan Martin Gonzalez is a 23-year-old back-rower for the Argentinian Pumas. He was a member of the Jaguares' Super Rugby AU title-winning team in 2020 and made his Pumas debut at the age of 19. He is known for his powerful carrying, skillful handling, and ability to adapt to different roles.

Juan Martin Gonzalez

64

Davit Niniashvili (Georgia)

Davit Niniashvili is a 22-year-old center for the Georgian Lelos. He was a member of the European Rugby Challenge Cup 2021 winning team and made his Lelos debut at the age of 18. He is known for his passing skills, evasive running, and ability to break the line.

Kurt-Lee Arendse (South Africa)

Kurt-Lee Arendse is a 24-year-old wing for the South African Springboks. He was a member of the Sharks' Currie Cup Premier Division title-winning team in 2022 and made his Springboks debut at the age of 22. He scored three tries at Rugby World Cup 2023 and is known for his electrifying pace, and powerful finishing.

Davit Niniashvili

Kurt-Lee Arendse

By Stefano Delfrate - Autumn Nations Series '22- Italia vs Sudafrica-584.jpg, CC BY-SA 2.0, https://commons.wikimedia.org/w/index.php?curid=130019576

Marcos Moneta (Argentina)

Marcos Moneta is a 21-year-old fullback for the Argentinian Pumas. He was a Jaguares' Super Rugby AU title-winning team member in 2020 and made his Pumas debut at 19.

He scored two tries at the Rugby World Cup 2023 and is known for his electrifying pace and aerial prowess.

Romain Ntamack (France)

Romain Ntamack is a 23-year-old fly-half for the French Les Bleus. He was a member of the Stade Toulousain's Top 14 title-winning team in 2021 and the France Six Nations Championship 2022 winning squad.

He started all seven games for France at the Rugby World Cup in 2023 and is known for his composure, leadership, and game-management skills.

Marcos Moneta (Argentina)

Romain Ntamack (France)
By Société Générale - https://www.youtube.com/watch?v=xqhYrKSsBjo, CC BY 3.0, https://commons.wikimedia.org/w/index.php?curid=132588598

DID YOU KNOW?

Player Name	Country	Notable Achievement	Age at Achievement
Will Jordan	New Zealand	Youngest player to win World Rugby Breakthrough Player of the Year (2021)	23
Carter Gordon	Australia	Wallabies debut at age 20, one of the youngest players to represent Australia	20
Damian Penaud	France	Top try-scorer in Top 14 French rugby union championship (2022-23 season)	24
Louis Bielle-Biarrey	France	Key player for France at 2023 Rugby World Cup, started all seven games at age 22	22
Juan Martin Gonzalez	Argentina	Versatile play at 2023 Rugby World Cup, playing in backline and back-row positions at age 23	23
Davit Niniashvili	Georgia	Outstanding performance at 2023 Rugby World Cup, scored two tries at age 22	22
Kurt-Lee Arendse	South Africa	Electrifying pace and three tries at 2023 Rugby World Cup at age 24	24
Ethan van der Merwe	South Africa	Solid presence in Springboks' front row, starting all seven games at 2023 Rugby World Cup at age 22	22
Marcos Moneta	Argentina	Electrifying pace and aerial prowess, scored two tries at 2023 Rugby World Cup at age 21	21
Romain Ntamack	France	Composure, leadership, and game management at 2023 Rugby World Cup, started all seven games at age 23	23

7. INSPIRING COACHES AND MENTORS

- Sir Clive Woodward: Shaping England's Success
- Sir Graham Henry: The All Blacks' Mastermind
- Eddie Jones: England's Strategic Leader

SIR CLIVE WOODWARD: SHAPING ENGLAND'S SUCCESS

Dear young rugby enthusiasts, gather around and let me tell you a fascinating story about an incredible coach who transformed English rugby and inspired a generation of players. Today, we will get to know Sir Clive Woodward, the mastermind behind England's historic Rugby World Cup victory in 2003.

Sir Clive Woodward was more than just a coach; he was a visionary, motivator, and master tactician. He believed in the power of teamwork, preparation, and the undying spirit of the underdog. He saw the potential in English rugby, a team that hadn't won the World Cup since 1906, and he was determined to change that.

Woodward's approach was unconventional. He challenged the traditional rugby mindset, introducing new training methods, analyzing data, and emphasizing mental strength. He even brought in experts from other sports, including cricket and American football, to broaden the team's perspectives.

Under Woodward's guidance, England's rugby team underwent a complete transformation. They became a force to be reckoned with, playing with power, precision, and passion. They were no longer just a team but a family united by a shared goal.

And then came the moment of truth – the 2003 Rugby World Cup in Australia. England entered the tournament as underdogs, facing opponents like New Zealand and South Africa. But Woodward had instilled a belief in his players that they could achieve greatness.

Sir Clive Woodward

By Doha Stadium Plus Qatar from Doha, Qatar - Clive Woodward, CC BY 2.0, https://commons.wikimedia.org/w/index.php?curid=26450115

Match after match, England defied expectations, overcoming tough opponents and silencing their critics. They reached the final, facing the mighty Wallabies, the defending champions on their home soil.

The final was an intense affair, a clash of titans. England fought tooth and nail, never giving up, even when they were behind. And in the dying seconds of the game, with the score tied, Jonny Wilkinson, England's fly-half, stepped up and kicked the winning drop goal.

The stadium erupted in a sea of red and white, the roar of the English fans echoing through the night. England had done it. They had conquered the world, and Sir Clive Woodward, the architect of their success, was lifted onto the shoulders of his players, a symbol of their triumph.

Woodward's legacy isn't just about winning a trophy; it's about inspiring a generation of rugby players and fans. He demonstrated that anything is achievable with hard work, dedication, and unconventional thinking.

So, young rugby enthusiasts, as you start your rugby journey, remember Sir Clive Woodward's wise words: "Believe in yourselves, never give up, and always strive to be the best you can be."

Trivia Facts:
- Sir Clive Woodward's England team was the first to win the Rugby World Cup without losing a match.

- Woodward was knighted by Queen Elizabeth II in 2004 for his services to rugby.

- He is the only coach to have won the Rugby World Cup, the Heineken Cup, and the English Premiership.

- Woodward is a Fellow of the Institute of Directors and a member of the British Sports Council.

- He is also a co-founder of the Laureus World Sports Academy, an organization that recognizes and rewards sporting excellence.

SIR GRAHAM HENRY: THE ALL BLACKS' MASTERMIND

Young rugby enthusiasts gather around and listen to a tale of Sir Graham Henry, the legendary coach who led the New Zealand All Blacks to unprecedented heights and became an icon of the sport. Sir Graham Henry was a coach, psychologist, tactician, and motivator. He understood the All Blacks' legacy and the weight of expectations they carried, and he knew how to transform that pressure into fuel for their success. His approach was holistic, focusing on physical training, tactical strategies, mental conditioning, and team culture.

Henry's coaching philosophy was simple yet profound: play with heart, passion, and precision. He instilled in his players a sense of belief, a conviction that they could achieve anything they set their minds to. He taught them to play for each other, to trust each other, and never to give up.

Under Henry's guidance, the All Blacks transformed from a team that had struggled in recent World Cups to one that dominated the world stage. They became a force to be reckoned with, known for their relentless attacking style, unwavering defense, and uncanny ability to score tries from anywhere on the field.

In both the 2011 Rugby World Cup in New Zealand and the 2015 Rugby World Cup in England, the All Blacks entered the tournament with a target on their backs and immense pressure of expectations. But Henry had prepared them for this, instilling the resilience and mental fortitude to overcome any challenge. The All Blacks played with the passion and precision that Henry had instilled in them, leaving no doubt who the best team in the world was.

Their back-to-back World Cup victories were not just about winning trophies; they redefined the sport, set new standards of excellence, and inspired a generation of rugby players and fans. Henry's legacy is one of innovation, passion, and belief in the power of teamwork.

As you embark on your rugby journey, young enthusiasts, remember Sir Graham Henry's words: "Play with heart, play with passion, and play for each other."Gather around, young rugby enthusiasts, and let me tell you a tale of a legendary coach, a man who guided the New Zealand All Blacks to unprecedented heights and became an icon of the sport. Today, we will meet Sir Graham Henry, the mastermind behind the All Blacks' back-to-back Rugby World Cup victories in 2011 and 2015.

Sir Graham Henry wasn't just a coach; he was a psychologist, a tactician, a motivator. He understood the All Blacks' legacy and the weight of expectations they carried, and he knew how to transform that pressure into fuel for their success. His approach was holistic, focusing on physical training, tactical strategies, mental conditioning, and team culture.

Henry's coaching philosophy was simple yet profound: play with heart, play with passion, and play with precision. He instilled in his players a sense of belief, a conviction that they could achieve anything they set their minds to. He taught them to play for each other, to trust each other, and never to give up. Under Henry's guidance, the All Blacks transformed from a team that had struggled in recent World Cups to one that dominated the world stage. They became a force to be reckoned with, known for their relentless attacking style, unwavering defense, and uncanny ability to score tries from anywhere on the field.

And then came the moments of truth – the 2011 Rugby World Cup in New Zealand and the 2015 Rugby World Cup in England. The All Blacks entered both tournaments with a target on their backs, the pressure of expectations immense. But Henry had prepared them for this, instilling the resilience and mental fortitude to overcome any challenge.

In both World Cups, the All Blacks faced tough opponents, each match a nail-biting affair. But they never wavered, never lost sight of their goal. They played with the passion and precision that Henry had instilled in them, leaving no doubt who the best team in the world was. The All Blacks' back-to-back World Cup victories under Sir Graham Henry were not just about winning trophies; they were about redefining the sport, setting new standards of excellence, and inspiring a generation of rugby players and fans. Henry's legacy is one of innovation, passion, and belief in the power of teamwork.

So, young rugby enthusiasts, as you embark on your rugby journeys, remember Sir Graham Henry's words: "Play with heart, play with passion, and play for each other."

By Blackcat; original by the Government of New Zealand - This is a retouched picture, which means that it has been digitally altered from its original version. Modifications: cropped. The original can be viewed here: Jerry Mateparae and Graham Henry 2012.jpg: ., CC BY 3.0 nz, https://commons.wikimedia.org/w/index.php?curid=44981129

Sir Graham Henry

Trivia Facts:

- Sir Graham Henry is the only coach to have won the Rugby World Cup with two different countries (New Zealand and Australia).
- He is the only coach to have led a team to a Rugby World Cup victory on home soil.
- Henry was knighted by Queen Elizabeth II in 2012 for his services to rugby.
- He is the only coach to have won the Rugby World Cup, the Tri-Nations/Rugby Championship, and the Super Rugby title.
- Henry is a member of the World Rugby Hall of Fame and the International Rugby Hall of Fame.

EDDIE JONES: ENGLAND'S STRATEGIC LEADER

Young rugby enthusiasts, gather around and let me tell you about a coach who transformed the fortunes of English rugby. Eddie Jones is the mastermind behind England's resurgence, leading them to a Rugby World Cup final and capturing the hearts of fans worldwide.

Jones was not only a coach but also a motivator, tactician, and leader of men. He understood the potential of the English team and the weight of expectations they carried and knew how to channel that energy into a winning formula. His approach was meticulous, focusing on detailed analysis, data-driven strategies, and a ruthless mindset on the field.

Jones' coaching philosophy revolved around three fundamental principles: discipline, accuracy, and adaptability.

He instilled in his players a sense of responsibility, commitment to precision, and the ability to adjust their game plan to any opponent or situation. He taught them to think like a team, trust each other, and never underestimate their potential.

Under Jones' guidance, England's rugby team underwent a remarkable transformation. They became known for their watertight defense, clinical finishing, and ability to grind out victories in any conditions. They played with power, precision, and tactical nous, making them a formidable opponent for any team.

England defied expectations in the 2015 Rugby World Cup, overcoming tough opponents and reaching the final. Though they ultimately fell short against a legendary All Blacks side, their performance captured the nation and demonstrated the fruits of Jones' strategic leadership.

Jones' legacy is not just about winning matches but also about changing the culture of English rugby, instilling a winning mentality, and inspiring a generation of players and fans. He showed that hard work, dedication, and a strategic mind make anything possible.

So, young rugby enthusiasts, as you embark on your rugby journeys, remember Eddie Jones' words: "Discipline, accuracy, and adaptability – these are the cornerstones of success."

Trivia Facts:

- Eddie Jones is the only coach leading three countries (Australia, Japan, and England) to a Rugby World Cup knockout stage.

- He is the only coach to have won the Super Rugby title, the Japan Top League, and the Six Nations Championship.

- Jones was named World Rugby Coach of the Year in 2015 and 2019.

- He is a member of the World Rugby Hall of Fame and the Australian Rugby Hall of Fame.

- Jones is an Order of Australia recipient, one of the highest honors bestowed by the Australian government.

Eddie Jones

*By Belinda Lester - Flickr: Auction, CC BY-SA 2.0,
https://commons.wikimedia.org/w/index.php?curid=27569638*

DID YOU KNOW?

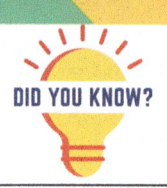

Coach	Nationality	Notable Achievement	Previous Profession(s)
Sir Clive Woodward	England	Mastermind behind England's 2003 Rugby World Cup victory	History Teacher at Plympton Grammar School in Devon, England
Sir Graham Henry	New Zealand	Led All Blacks to back-to-back World Cup titles (2011, 2015)	Successful Businessman
Eddie Jones	Australia	Led three different countries to Rugby World Cup knockout stages	Rugby Referee, Journalist
John Mitchell	South Africa	Led Springboks to third place at the 2003 Rugby World Cup	Physical Education Teacher, Rugby Player
Wayne Smith	New Zealand	Won numerous trophies with Canterbury and the Crusaders	Civil Engineer
Jake White	South Africa	Led Springboks to a surprise victory at the 2007 Rugby World Cup	School Teacher, Rugby Coach
Warren Gatland	New Zealand	Led Wales and the British and Irish Lions to numerous victories	High School Rugby Coach in Hamilton, New Zealand
Jacques Brunel	France	Led Les Bleus to the 2011 Rugby World Cup final	Successful Club Coach in France
Michael Cheika	Australia	Led Wallabies to the 2015 Rugby World Cup final	Professional Rugby League Player
Fabien Galthié	France	Former France international and current Les Bleus coach	Successful Business Consultant
Dave Rennie	Australia	Led the Scotland national team to new heights	Successful Club Coach in New Zealand and Australia
Jamie Joseph	New Zealand	Former Japan international and current Brave Blossoms coach	Successful Club Coach in New Zealand and Japan

8. THE GLOBAL RUGBY FAMILY

- The Spirit of Rugby World Cups
- The Passion of the Six Nations
- The Thrill of the Rugby Championship

THE SPIRIT OF RUGBY WORLD CUPS

Welcome, young rugby enthusiasts! Let me take you on a journey through the most prestigious tournament in rugby - the Rugby World Cup. It's a tale of passion, unity, and the spirit of the game that transcends borders and unites people from all corners of the globe.

The Rugby World Cup brings together the best rugby nations every four years. Each team has its unique style, traditions, and dreams of glory. It's a stage where legends are born, underdogs rise, and the spirit of rugby shines brightest.

The Rugby World Cup is not only about winning trophies or scoring tries; it's about the camaraderie, the sportsmanship, and the shared love for the game that binds us together. Fans travel far and wide to support their teams, volunteers give their time and energy, and players put their hearts and souls on the field, representing their nations with pride.

I've witnessed the magic of the Rugby World Cup firsthand. I experienced the electrifying atmosphere in stadiums, the passionate cheers of supporters, and the outpouring of emotions after every match. It's a celebration of rugby that transcends the game itself, bringing people together from all walks of life, united by their love for the sport.

Let me share some of the most memorable moments from the Rugby World Cup's history. These moments encapsulate the game's spirit and its fans' passion.

In 1995, at the inaugural Rugby World Cup in South Africa, Jonah Lomu, a young and powerful Fijian winger, burst onto the scene with four tries against England, etching his name in rugby history and inspiring a generation of players.

In 2003, in the final moments of a thrilling match against Australia, England's Jonny Wilkinson stepped up and kicked a drop goal, snatching victory from the jaws of defeat and sending the home crowd into a frenzy.

In 2015, the Japanese rugby team, known as the Brave Blossoms, defied expectations by defeating South Africa, a rugby powerhouse, in one of the biggest upsets in sporting history. The victory sent shockwaves through the rugby world and captured the hearts of fans everywhere.

The Rugby World Cup is more than just a competition; it symbolizes global unity and sportsmanship. It brings together the best rugby nations from all corners of the world, showcasing the diversity and talent of the sport. It's a platform for countries to showcase their cultures, traditions, and passion for rugby.

The tournament's legacy extends beyond the field, inspiring generations of rugby players and fans worldwide. It teaches us about teamwork, respect, resilience, and the importance of sportsmanship. It reminds us that no matter where we come from, we can all share the joy of rugby and the spirit of competition.

So, young rugby enthusiasts, remember the lessons of the Rugby World Cup as you embark on your own rugby journeys. Carry the spirit of the game with you, embrace the diversity of the rugby family, and always play with passion, integrity, and respect.

Remember, the Rugby World Cup is more than just a tournament; it's a celebration of rugby, a symbol of unity, and a source of inspiration. It's a reminder of the power of sport to bring people together and create unforgettable moments.

World Cup: Did You Know?

- The first Rugby World Cup was held in 1987, with New Zealand emerging as the inaugural champions.

- The tournament has been held every four years since 1987, with New Zealand and South Africa winning the title three times, Australia twice, and England once.

- The Rugby World Cup has grown from 16 teams in 1987 to 20 in the current format.

- The Rugby World Cup is the third most-watched sporting event in the world, after the Olympic Games and the FIFA World Cup.

- The Rugby World Cup is known for its passionate fan base, who travel in large numbers to support their teams.

- The tournament has produced some of the most iconic moments in rugby history, such as Jonah Lomu's four tries against England in 1995 and Jonny Wilkinson's drop goal to win the 2003 World Cup final.

- The Rugby World Cup has played a significant role in promoting rugby worldwide, helping to grow the sport's popularity and reach new audiences.

- The tournament has also positively impacted host countries, boosting tourism and economic development.

- The Rugby World Cup symbolizes global unity and sportsmanship, bringing together the best rugby nations from all corners of the world.

- The tournament's legacy extends beyond the field, inspiring generations of rugby players and fans worldwide.

Rugby World Cup

By Carrington & Co, London (trophy, based on the cup and cover by Paul de Lamerie)Roman.b (derivative work) - Own work, Public Domain, https://commons.wikimedia.org/w/index.php?curid=22210815

THE PASSION OF THE SIX NATIONS

Hey there, young rugby fans! Let me guide you through one of the world's most exciting and significant rugby tournaments - the Six Nations Championship.

For more than a hundred years, this competition has been engaging audiences with its intense rivalries, impressive displays of skill, and the electrifying atmosphere surrounding every match. Let's dive into Six Nations' captivating world and experience the game's thrill together!

The Six Nations Championship is a clash of titans, bringing together six of the most renowned rugby nations: England, France, Ireland, Italy, Scotland, and Wales. Each team has a rich rugby heritage, a unique playing style, and a genuine fan base that adds to the tournament's electrifying energy.

Imagine packed stadiums filled with the crowd's roar as the teams clash on the field, wearing the colors of their proud nations. The passion and intensity are palpable, and the air is thick with anticipation and excitement.

Over the years, the Six Nations Championship has produced countless unforgettable moments etched into rugby folklore. Think of Will Greenwood's barnstorming try for England against Ireland in 2003 or Chris Paterson's dramatic drop goal to secure victory for Scotland against France in 2001.

These moments, and countless others, have defined the tournament's legacy and ignited fans' passion worldwide.

However, the Six Nations isn't just about the drama and spectacle; it's also about the camaraderie, the respect, and the shared love for the game that binds these six rugby nations together. Players from rival teams become teammates when they represent their British and Irish Lions, showcasing the unity and spirit of sportsmanship that transcends borders and rivalries.

So, young rugby enthusiasts, as you embark on your rugby journeys, let the Six Nations Championship inspire you. Embrace the passion, the teamwork, and the unwavering dedication that make this tournament unique. Remember, rugby is more than just a game; it's a celebration of the human spirit, a symbol of unity, and a source of endless inspiration.

Did You Know:

- The Six Nations Championship originated from the Home Nations Championship, contested between England, Ireland, Scotland, and Wales from 1883 to 1909.

- France joined the tournament in 1910, forming the Five Nations Championship until 2000.

- Italy joined the tournament in 2000, expanding it to the current Six Nations format.

- The Six Nations Championship is the world's oldest international rugby union competition.

- England, with 39 titles, is the most successful team in the history of the Six Nations Championship.

- Scotland's Calcutta Cup against England is one of the oldest rivalries in rugby, dating back to 1872.

- Ireland's Triple Crown, achieved by winning all three home matches against England, Scotland, and Wales, is a coveted honor.

- France's Grand Slam, achieved by winning all five matches in the tournament, is a symbol of dominance.

- Italy's first Six Nations victory, against Scotland in 2000, was a historic moment for the team and the tournament.

- The Six Nations Championship significantly impacts the global rugby calendar, influencing the rankings and seeding of international teams.

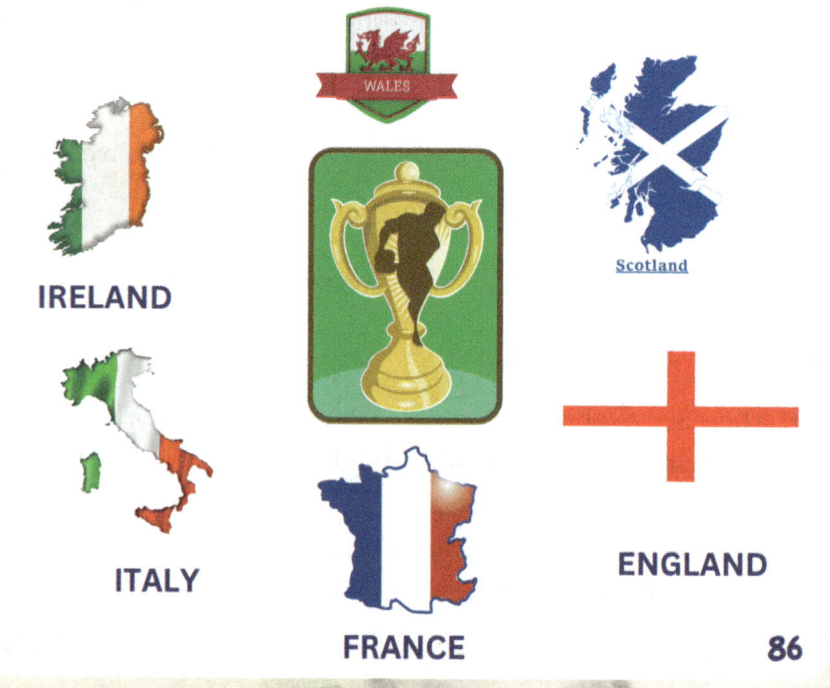

IRELAND

Scotland

ITALY

FRANCE

ENGLAND

THE THRILL OF THE RUGBY CHAMPIONSHIP

Welcome, young rugby enthusiasts, to the southern hemisphere, where rugby is more than just a game; it's a passion. In this Rugby Championship, four of the world's most formidable rugby nations – Argentina, Australia, New Zealand, and South Africa – compete for supremacy on the field, showcasing their unique styles of play, unwavering determination, and deep-rooted love for the game.

Picture the scene – the sun-kissed stadiums of Argentina, Australia, New Zealand, and South Africa, alive with the roar of passionate fans, their voices echoing the fierce competition unfolding on the field. The players, dressed in their national jerseys, embody the pride and spirit of their countries, with every move met with cheers and gasps of anticipation.

The Rugby Championship isn't just about winning or losing; it's about celebrating the diversity of rugby, the resilience of its players, and the shared love for the game that unites people from all corners of the world. It's a testament to the power of sport to transcend borders, foster camaraderie, and inspire generations of rugby enthusiasts.

Let me share some exciting anecdotes from the tournament's history that have defined its legacy and ignited fans' passion worldwide:

In 2015, the Pumas of Argentina, known for their underdog spirit, surprised everyone by defeating the mighty All Blacks of New Zealand, proving that anything is possible on the rugby field.

In 2011, the Wallabies of Australia, led by their captain and scrum-half, Will Genia, produced a miraculous comeback victory against the Springboks of South Africa in the Rugby World Cup final, showcasing their never-say-die attitude and the resilience of the Australian rugby spirit.

In 2007, the Springboks of South Africa, facing immense pressure and expectations as hosts of the Rugby World Cup, rose to the occasion and lifted the Webb Ellis Cup, demonstrating their unwavering determination and the power of home support.

In 1987, the All Blacks of New Zealand, led by their legendary captain, David Kirk, made history by becoming the first Rugby World Cup champions, setting a benchmark for excellence and inspiring rugby players worldwide.

These anecdotes, and many more, have defined the tournament's legacy and sparked fans' passion worldwide. They remind us that rugby is more than just a game; it's about teamwork, respect, resilience, and the spirit of competition.

So, young rugby enthusiasts, let the Rugby Championship inspire you as you embark on your rugby journeys. Embrace the diversity of the rugby world, the spirit of teamwork, and the unwavering dedication that makes this tournament so unique.

Remember, rugby is more than just a game; it's a celebration of the human spirit, a symbol of unity, and a source of endless inspiration.

Did You Know:

- The Rugby Championship originated from the Tri-Nations Series, contested between Australia, New Zealand, and South Africa from 1996 to 2011.

- Argentina joined the tournament in 2012, expanding it to the current Rugby Championship format.

- New Zealand, with 18 titles, is the most successful team in the history of the Rugby Championship.

- The Bledisloe Cup, contested between Australia and New Zealand, is one of the most intense rivalries in rugby.

- The Pumas' passion and fighting spirit have made them a force to be reckoned with in the Rugby Championship.

- The Wallabies' attacking flair and determination have captivated fans worldwide.

- The Springboks' physicality and resilience have earned them a reputation as one of the toughest teams in rugby.

- The Rugby Championship has played a significant role in promoting rugby in the southern hemisphere, helping to grow the sport's popularity and reach new audiences.

- The tournament has also positively impacted host countries, boosting tourism and economic development.

- The Rugby Championship symbolizes global unity and sportsmanship, bringing together four of the world's best rugby nations.

A South African line-out against New Zealand in 2006

By Hamish McConnochie, Attribution, https://commons.wikimedia.org/w/index.php?curid=16267391

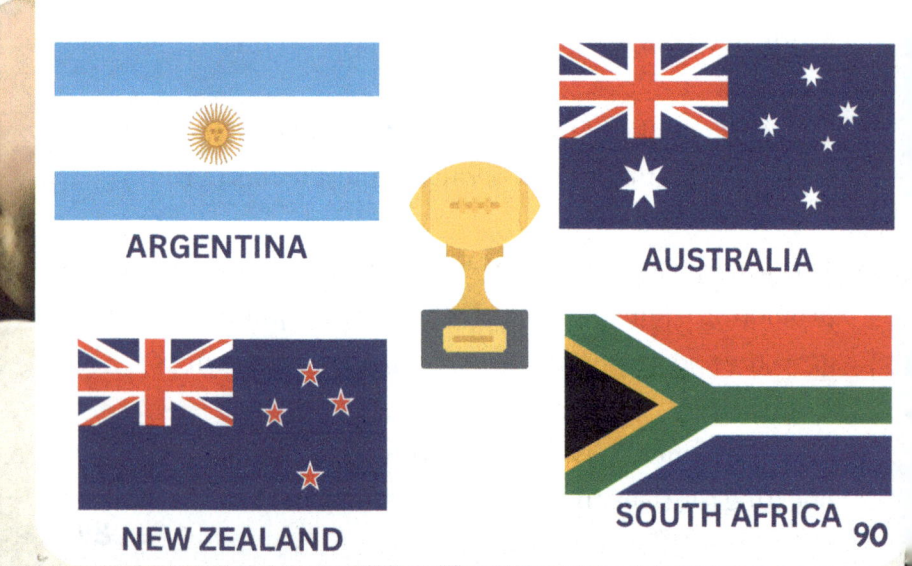

ARGENTINA

AUSTRALIA

NEW ZEALAND

SOUTH AFRICA

90

DID YOU KNOW?

Year	Event	Details
1987	1987 Rugby World Cup	The Italian team was given the wrong jerseys and had to play in blue instead of their traditional blue and white.
1995	1995 Rugby World Cup	A group of South African fans painted a cow in the colors of the Springboks national team and drove it around the stadium before the final match.
2003	2003 Rugby World Cup	Jonny Wilkinson famously kicked a drop goal to win the final against Australia, admitting later that he had no idea how he did it.
2011	2011 Rugby World Cup	The All Blacks performed their traditional haka, and the Argentinian players responded by doing their own version of the haka, catching the All Blacks off guard.
2015	2015 Rugby World Cup	The Japanese team, known as the Brave Blossoms, shocked the world by defeating South Africa in a major upset.
2019	2019 Rugby World Cup	Wales celebrated their victory over Australia by singing their national anthem, "Land of My Fathers," in the middle of the stadium.
2023	2023 Rugby World Cup	The South African team performed a special version of their traditional war cry, the "Jerusalema," with popular musician Master KG.
-	Six Nations Championship	Known for passionate rivalries, one of the most famous is the Calcutta Cup, contested between England and Scotland.
-	Rugby Championship	Known for its physicality, the "Battle of Brisbane" in 2011 was a particularly brutal match between Australia and New Zealand.
-	General Fact	Rugby is enjoyed by people of all ages and abilities, and there is even a category for dwarves, who play a special version of the game called "dwarf rugby."

9. QUIZ TIME

How well you know the game!

Quiz Time

1. Who kicked the drop goal that won England the 2003 Rugby World Cup final?

(A) Jonny Wilkinson (B) Clive Woodward (C) Martin Johnson (D) Jonah Lomu

2. Which New Zealand rugby legend was known for his incredible power and speed?

(A) Richie McCaw (B) Jonah Lomu (C) Gareth Edwards (D) Jonny Wilkinson

3. Who was the Welsh rugby player nicknamed "The Maestro" for his exceptional passing skills?

(A) Jonny Wilkinson (B) Clive Woodward (C) Martin Johnson (D) Gareth Edwards

4. Which rugby match is often referred to as "the greatest test match ever played"?

(A) The 2003 Rugby World Cup Final: England vs. Australia
(B) The 'Invincible' Tour of the British and Irish Lions
(C) The 1973 Barbarians vs. All Blacks Match: A Try for the Ages
(D) The 2015 Rugby World Cup Final: New Zealand vs. Australia

Quiz Time

5. In which year did the British and Irish Lions embark on their famous 'Invincible' Tour, remaining undefeated against all opposition?

(A) 1971 (B) 1989 (C) 1997 (D) 2005

6. Which match featured the iconic "Try for the Ages" scored by Gareth Edwards for the Barbarians against the All Blacks in 1973?

(A) The 2003 Rugby World Cup Final: England vs. Australia (B) The 'Invincible' Tour of the British and Irish Lions (C) The 1973 Barbarians vs. All Blacks Match: A Try for the Ages (D) The 1995 Rugby World Cup Final: South Africa vs. New Zealand

7. Who captained England to victory in the 2003 Rugby World Cup and is considered one of the greatest English rugby players of all time?

(A) Jonny Wilkinson (B) Clive Woodward (C) Martin Johnson (D) Jonah Lomu

8. Which rugby rivalry is known for its fierce competition and is contested annually between England and Scotland in the Six Nations Championship?

(A) The Calcutta Cup (B) The Bledisloe Cup (C) The Webb Ellis Cup (D) The Mandela Cup

Quiz Time

9. Which Australian rugby player is known for his strong social activism and advocacy for human rights?

(A)David Pocock (B) Billy Vunipola (C) James O'Connor (D) Richie McCaw

10. Which English rugby player is considered one of the most decorated female players of all time, having won multiple World Cups and Olympic medals?

(A)Emily Scarratt (B)Richie McCaw (C) David Pocock (D) Jonah Lomu

11. Which New Zealand women's rugby team is known for its dominance in international rugby, having won multiple World Cups and remained undefeated for over 17 years?

(A)The Wallaroos (B) The Black Ferns (C)The Red Roses (D) The XV de France

12. Which team achieved a historic upset by defeating South Africa, a rugby powerhouse, in the 2015 Rugby World Cup?

(A) Japan (B) England (C)Australia (D) New Zealand

Quiz Time

13. Which English rugby anthem, known for its uplifting lyrics and spirit of camaraderie, is often sung by fans before and after matches?

(A) "God Save the Queen" (B)"Jerusalem" (C)"Rule, Britannia!" (D)"Swing Low, Sweet Chariot"

14. Which New Zealand rugby legend is known for his exceptional leadership, resilience, and contributions to the game?

(A) Richie McCaw (B)Jonah Lomu (C)Gareth Edwards (D)Billy Vunipola

15. Which English rugby player is considered a rising star in English rugby, known for his powerful running and tackling?

(A) Billy Vunipola (B)James O'Connor (C)David Pocock (D)Richie McCaw

16. Which Australian rugby player is known for his remarkable comeback from injuries and his determination to succeed?

(A) Billy Vunipola (B)James O'Connor (C)David Pocock (D)Richie McCaw

Quiz Time

17. Which British rugby coach led England to their 2003 Rugby World Cup triumph and is considered a mastermind of the game?

(A) Sir Clive Woodward (B)Sir Graham Henry (C)Eddie Jones (D)Richie McCaw

18. Which New Zealand rugby coach led the All Blacks to their three consecutive Rugby World Cup titles and is widely regarded as one of the greatest coaches of all time?

(A) Sir Clive Woodward (B) Eddie Jones (C)Gareth Edwards (D)Sir Graham Henry

19. Which English rugby coach is known for his innovative and strategic approach to the game, leading England to their 2019 Rugby World Cup final?

(A) Sir Clive Woodward (B)Sir Graham Henry (C)Eddie Jones (D) Richie McCaw

20. Which major rugby tournament brings together the four powerhouse nations of the Southern Hemisphere: Argentina, Australia, New Zealand, and South Africa?

(A) The Rugby World Cup (B)The Six Nations Championship (C) The Rugby Championship (D)The British and Irish Lions Tour

Quiz Time

21. Which rugby tradition involves the players and fans joining together in a powerful and unifying chant or song before the start of matches?

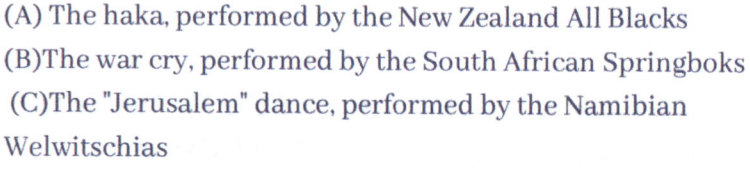

(A) The haka, performed by the New Zealand All Blacks
(B) The war cry, performed by the South African Springboks
(C) The "Jerusalem" dance, performed by the Namibian Welwitschias
(D) All of the above

22. Which annual rugby tournament showcases the fierce rivalry between England, Scotland, Wales, Ireland, France, and Italy?

(A) The Rugby World Cup (B) The Six Nations Championship
(C) The Rugby Championship (D) The British and Irish Lions Tour

Fun Corner-Answer

Fun Corner 1

- Which country has won the most Rugby World Cups?
  Answer: New Zealand
- What is the name of the trophy awarded to the Six Nations Championship winner?
  Answer: The Calcutta Cup
- Who is the all-time leading try scorer in Rugby World Cup history?
  Answer: Bryan Habana (South Africa)

Fun Corner 2

- Which Welsh rugby player captained his team to three Grand Slams in the 1970s and is often referred to as "The Maestro of Welsh Rugby"?
  Answer: Gareth Edwards
- Who is known for his meticulous kicking technique and secured England's victory in the 2003 Rugby World Cup final with a crucial drop goal?
  Answer: Jonny Wilkinson
- In 1971, which legendary player scored a breathtaking try during a British Lions tour of New Zealand, covering over 100 meters and weaving through the All Blacks defense?
  Answer: Gareth Edwards

Quiz Time-Answer

1. (A) Jonny Wilkinson
2. (B) Jonah Lomu
3. (D) Gareth Edwards
4. (A) The 2003 Rugby World Cup Final: England vs. Australia
5. (A) 1971
6. (C) The 1973 Barbarians vs. All Blacks Match: A Try for the Ages
7. (C) Martin Johnson
8. (A) The Calcutta Cup
9. (A) David Pocock
10. (A) Emily Scarratt
11. (B) The Black Ferns
12. (A) Japan
13. (D) "Swing Low, Sweet Chariot"
14. (A) Richie McCaw
15. (A) Billy Vunipola
16. (B) James O'Connor
17. (A) Sir Clive Woodward
18. (D) Sir Graham Henry
19. (C) Eddie Jones
20. (C) The Rugby Championship
21. (D) All of the above
22. (B) The Six Nations Championship

We'd Love Your Feedback!

⭐⭐⭐⭐⭐

Please let us know how we're doing by leaving us a review.

CONCLUSION

As we end our journey through the world of rugby, we are left with a profound appreciation for the sport's unique blend of athleticism, camaraderie, and sportsmanship. We have witnessed the triumphs and tribulations of legendary players, the passion of unforgettable matches, and the inspiring stories of those who have overcome adversity to achieve greatness.

Rugby is more than just a game; it's a tapestry woven with threads of courage, determination, and respect. It's a sport that teaches us the value of teamwork, the importance of sportsmanship, and the resilience of the human spirit.

As young readers embark on their rugby journeys, whether as players, fans, or simply admirers of the sport, let these stories serve as beacons of inspiration. Remember that the true essence of rugby lies not just in winning or losing but in the spirit in which the game is played.

May you carry the lessons learned from these inspiring tales, embrace the challenges, cherish the victories, and always strive to embody the values of rugby: integrity, passion, and respect.

Thank you for joining me on this incredible journey through the world of rugby. May the spirit of the game continue to ignite your passions and inspire you to reach for your dreams.

Good luck with your rugby adventure!

Dr. Fanatomy

CHECK MY OTHER BOOKS .....

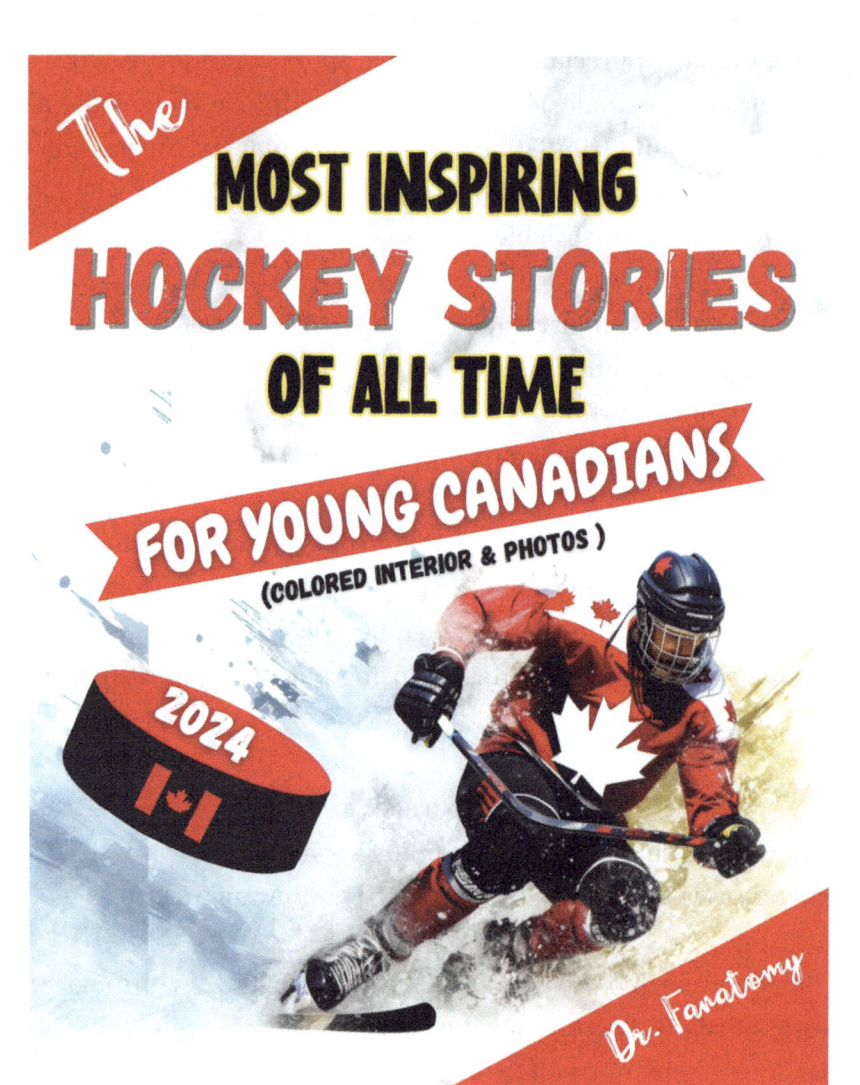

The MOST INSPIRING HOCKEY STORIES OF ALL TIME FOR YOUNG CANADIANS

(COLORED INTERIOR & PHOTOS)

2024

Dr. Fanatomy

Made in United States
North Haven, CT
02 December 2024